THE EVERLASTING CHECK

The Everlasting Check

HUME ON MIRACLES

Alexander George

Harvard University Press   Cambridge, Massachusetts · London, England   2016

First printing

"Once in a Lifetime": Words and music by Brian Eno, David Byrne,
Christopher Frantz, Jerry Harrison, and Tina Weymouth.
Copyright © 1980 by EG Music Ltd., WB Music Corp., and Index
Music, Inc. All rights for EG Music Ltd. in the United States and
Canada administered by Universal Music–MGB Songs. All rights
for Index Music, Inc., administered by WB Music Corp.
International copyright secured. All rights reserved. Reprinted by
permission of Hal Leonard Corporation.

Epigraph: From Ludwig Wittgenstein, *Philosophical Investigations,*
3rd ed., trans. G. E. M. Anscombe (New York: Macmillan, 1968),
§481.

Library of Congress Cataloging-in-Publication Data
George, Alexander.
    The everlasting check : Hume on miracles / Alexander George.
        pages cm
    Includes index.
    ISBN 978-0-674-28924-6 (hardcover)
1. Hume, David, 1711–1776. 2. Miracles. I. Title.
    B1499.M5G46 2015
    212—dc23   2015013303

To E., a miracle

My sheep hear my voice.

—John 10:27 (King James)

If anyone said that information about the past could not convince him
that something would happen in the future,
I should not understand him.

—Ludwig Wittgenstein, *Philosophical Investigations,* §481

CONTENTS

PREFACE

One day in 1734, while walking in the cloisters of the Jesuits' College at La Flèche near Anjou in France, engaged in a conversation with a Jesuit about "some nonsensical miracle performed in their convent," a young David Hume was struck by a *reason* for being doubtful. This "argument immediately occurred to me, and I thought it very much gravelled my companion," Hume reported. "[B]ut at last he observed to me that it was impossible for that argument to have any solidity, because it operated equally against the Gospel as the Catholic miracles;—which observation I thought proper to admit as a sufficient answer."[1]

---

1. Letter 194, to the Rev. George Campbell, 7 June 1762, in *The Letters of David Hume*, Volume 1, J. Y. T. Greig (editor), Oxford, 1932, pp. 360-61; p. 361. Hume concluded in full throttle: "I believe you will allow, that the freedom at least of this reasoning makes it

Hume's companion has not been alone in questioning the cogency of Hume's skeptical argument about miracles: the argument—what it is meant to show and whether it succeeds in doing so—has never ceased to generate heated commentary. In what follows, I shall articulate the thesis and the argument that Hume truly intended. I believe that his actual argument is philosophically rich and far more robust than is generally thought. Its interest extends much beyond the local issue of miracles. Indeed, this is one reason why his argument has garnered such philosophical scrutiny through the centuries: it quickly raises central issues about justification, rationality, and language. Once it is firmly in place, clearly articulated, and brought into focus by consideration of a number of classical interpretations and objections, I shall have something to say about what we should make of it, especially in the context of some remarks by Ludwig Wittgenstein on magic, ritual, and religion.

Some disclaimers are in order, however. With more than two-and-a-half centuries of commentary behind us, it would be presumptuous to pretend to a thoroughgoing originality: as Hume said *à propos* something else, "New discoveries are not to be expected in these matters."[2] I also do not aim for a comprehensive interpretation, for there are facets of Hume's discussion on which I will not comment and alternative interpretations with which I will not take issue. Finally, I have no wish to defend Hume, as I interpret him, against all attacks: I do find that many of these are mistaken, but I will consider only some representative objections, largely with a view to clarifying Hume's thesis and demonstrating the interest and power of his argument.

I do believe that even a very informed reader will find, as chess players like to put it, novelties here. And I should like to think that, even if each element of my interpretation were to have been advanced by someone, no one to date has assembled them all into a single, unified account. Furthermore, it seems to me that some of the big ideas in Hume's discussion—ones that I think he was pleased to have hit upon and to have interestingly stitched together—are often missed, and that a

---

somewhat extraordinary to have been the produce of a convent of Jesuits, tho perhaps you may think the sophistry of it savours plainly of the place of its birth."

2. "Of the Social Contract," reprinted in *Essays: Moral, Political, and Literary* (revised edition), Eugene F. Miller (editor), Liberty Fund, 1987, pp. 465–87; p. 487.

compact yet textured presentation of his argument's conclusion and architecture will be of value.

Hume himself was in no doubt about the potency of his argument. He was originally going to include it in *A Treatise of Human Nature,* but then feared that it would "give too much offence." And so he resigned himself to "castrating my work, that is, cutting off its noble parts": the *Treatise* was published without any mention of his argument.[3] These "noble parts" finally saw the light of day in 1748, as Section 10 of *An Enquiry Concerning Human Understanding*: "Of Miracles."

3. Letter 1, to Henry Home, 2 December 1737, in *New Letters of David Hume,* Raymond Klibansky and Ernest C. Mossner (editors), Oxford, 1954, pp. 1-3; p. 3.

1

HUME'S MIRACLES

1.1. Interpretative difficulties begin with the essay's title: what does Hume mean by "miracle"? Given that Hume explicitly tells us what he means, this is more vexing than one might expect: "A miracle," he says, "is a violation of the laws of nature."[1] On its face, this characterization immediately rules miracles out of existence by linguistic fiat. If a law of nature is a true description of some natural regularity—say, of the form, "Whenever something of this kind happens, something of that kind happens"—then there could not be events that fail to conform to a law. If

---

1. "Of Miracles," in *An Enquiry Concerning Human Understanding* (critical edition), Tom L. Beauchamp (editor), Oxford, 2006, pp. 83–99; paragraph 12. Hume frequently puts the matter this way. In note 3, for instance, he talks of a miracle as something "contrary to the laws of nature" and as a "transgression of these laws."

to call something a law is to say that it correctly describes some pattern in the world—that is, that no events contravene it—then there simply are no miracles (as Hume here characterizes them) with respect to that law.

Another way to make the same point is to highlight the self-subverting nature of the claim that a miracle, so understood, has occurred. Assume that an event is a miracle. It then follows that there exists a law of nature that the event violates. But if a law is a correct description of the world, then there exists a description of the world that is both correct and incorrect, an absurdity. Hence, the event fails to be a miracle after all. By *reductio ad absurdum*, there are no miracles.[2]

Some, like Spinoza, have thought this the correct position to take concerning miracles. Many have suspected this is the argument that Hume ultimately relies on in his critique of miracles.[3] And yet this cannot be anything like Hume's argument. In "Of Miracles," he divides

---

2. Many commentators simply repeat Hume's definition without mentioning the difficulty a straight reading presents. For instance, Tom L. Beauchamp writes that for Hume, "miraculous events must actually violate a law," which is "a perfectly uniform causal regularity in nature." "A miracle," he says, "violates a law by not conforming to a universal regularity" (*An Enquiry Concerning Human Understanding* [student edition], Oxford, 1999, pp. 45, 247). Beauchamp does not address how a "perfectly uniform" or "universal" regularity could possibly be violated.

Others make the difficulty explicit but seek to defuse it by somehow imagining that Hume thought a regularity's status as a law of nature could withstand a single exception. (See, for instance, C. D. Broad, "Hume's Theory of the Credibility of Miracles," *Proceedings of the Aristotelian Society,* 1916–17, pp. 77–94; p. 86.)

Pursuing a different but no less drastic line, some commentators argue that Hume misrepresents his own conception of miracle, which rather has to do with the causal pedigree of an event: should the event be caused by God, or by a divine envoy, then it is a miracle; otherwise, it is not. (A reading of this kind is advanced by, for instance, Norman Kemp Smith; see his edition of *Hume's Dialogues Concerning Natural Religion* [second edition], Social Sciences Publishers, 1948, p. 48.) Such interpretations are also completely unsatisfactory. An event that is caused by God might be one that we expect very strongly: the billiard ball's motion might be due to God's interposition rather than to the fact that it was struck by another ball. On this interpretation, therefore, we could not move from the assumption that an event is a miracle to any conclusions about how it runs counter to our past experiences—yet, as we shall see, such a move is at the heart of Hume's argument.

Yet others accept this consequence of a straight reading of Hume's definition and instead present it as the core of Hume's argument against miracles; see the text's following paragraph and footnote 6.

3. See, for instance. Robert J. Fogelin's "What Hume Actually Said about Miracles," *Hume Studies,* vol. 16, no. 1, 1990, pp. 81–86; David Fate Norton's *David Hume: Common-Sense Moralist, Sceptical Metaphysician,* Princeton, 1982, p. 82; or John Earman's *Hume's Abject Failure: The Argument Against Miracles,* Oxford, 2000.

his presentation into two parts, and both are shot through with empirical considerations. It would be impossible to explain why Hume extends his discussion over forty-one paragraphs and appeals to many facts about human psychology and history if he thought he had at his disposal an argument against miracles that could be presented in a single paragraph.

We can make interpretative progress if we temporarily turn away from Hume's explicit definitions and instead attend to the conditions under which he actually employs the term *miracle*. Hume says:

> It is no miracle that a man, seemingly in good health, should die on a sudden; because such a kind of death, though more unusual than any other, has yet been frequently observed to happen. But it is a miracle, that a dead man should come to life; because that has never been observed, in any age or country.[4]

Here, the critical consideration in determining whether an event is a miracle is whether it conflicts with a very well-confirmed regularity, one for which we have a tremendous amount of observational evidence.[5] The conflict is with our present judgment about what the laws of nature are, not with the laws themselves; put otherwise, the conflict is not with a law of nature but with a well-confirmed candidate for such a law.

This thought is supported by other passages in Hume's discussion. Consider, for instance, his claim that "[t]here must, therefore, be a uniform experience against every miraculous event, *otherwise the event would not merit that appellation*."[6] What gives one the right to call an event "miraculous" is that it violates a well-confirmed description of the world. Following Nelson Goodman, let us say that a statement is *lawlike* if it has all the requisite attributes of a law save perhaps for truth.[7] We can then say that a miracle, for Hume, is an event that conflicts with a well-confirmed lawlike statement.[8]

---

4. "Of Miracles," paragraph 12.
5. Here and elsewhere, I do not scruple to write of events (rather than of propositional descriptions of them) conflicting with statements.
6. "Of Miracles," paragraph 12, emphasis added.
7. See Goodman's *Fact, Fiction, and Forecast* (fourth edition), Harvard, 1983, p. 22.
8. It is natural to wonder why, given this epistemic conception of a miracle, Hume's views on induction do not immediately lead to the conclusion that there are no miracles: for if those views entail that there are no well-confirmed lawlike statements, then of course no

How well confirmed the lawlike statement has to be in order to make a violation of it a miracle is something to which I shall turn in a moment. For now, note that a consequence of this conception is that it makes sense to talk of an event's being more or less miraculous: as the confirmation of a lawlike statement increases, an event that violates it becomes more of a miracle. If instead we were to take miracles to be violations of natural law, understood in a straightforward fashion, such a graduated construal of miracles would be difficult to understand: either an event is such a violation or it is not, and whether it is should be independent of the level of confirmation for the lawlike statement with which it conflicts. Yet Hume does give voice to precisely such a graduated conception when he writes of one event's being "more miraculous" than another or of one event's being "the greater miracle."[9]

If one takes Hume's explicit definition of "miracle" flatly, then one will also have a difficult time making sense of his talk of marvelous events and their contrast with miracles. He writes, for instance, that "in order to encrease the probability against the testimony of witnesses, let us suppose, that the fact, which they affirm, instead of being only marvelous, is really miraculous."[10] Why should an event's being miraculous rather than merely marvelous have the consequence that the probability of the incorrectness of testimony on its behalf increases? However, this does follow if we assume, first, that the probability of the testimony's incorrectness increases with the probability that the lawlike statement the witnessed event violates is correct and, second, that the probability of correctness of a lawlike claim with which a miracle conflicts is greater than the probability of correctness of a lawlike claim with which a merely marvelous event conflicts. On this natural reading of Hume, the difference between a marvelous event and a miraculous one is indeed a matter of degree: as the evidence in favor of a lawlike statement increases, a violation of it moves from being merely extraordinary, to marvelous, and finally, to miraculous.[11]

---

events conflict with such a statement—that is, no events are miracles. The question raises interesting issues, and I shall return to it at a more helpful juncture below.

9. "Of Miracles," paragraph 13.

10. "Of Miracles," paragraph 11.

11. Beauchamp writes: "Miraculous events must actually violate a law—that is, a causal regularity in nature—whereas the 'marvelous' merely violates *expectations* of lawful

If a miracle were a violation of a law of nature, there would be no link between an event's being miraculous and the strength of our evidence against it. For we may have no idea that a given statement expresses a law of nature and so no idea that some particular event, which indeed violates it, is a miracle. Thus, from an event's being a miracle, nothing could be inferred about the strength of our evidence against the correctness of testimony on its behalf. And yet as we shall see, this is a move that Hume makes throughout his discussion. By contrast, if to call something a miracle—to say it "merits that appellation"— is just to say that evidence of a certain weight exists against it, then it immediately follows that evidence of a certain weight exists against the correctness of testimony on its behalf.

Some passages might encourage the thought that Hume takes the notion of "miracle" to be nonepistemic. For instance, in the following, one might read Hume as saying that whether an event is a miracle is independent of our beliefs:

> A miracle may either be discoverable by men or not. This alters not its nature and essence. The raising of a house or a ship into the air is a visible miracle. The raising of a feather, when the wind wants ever so little of a force requisite for that purpose, is as real a miracle, though not so sensible with regard to us.[12]

But this would be to misunderstand the independence in question. What Hume claims here is simply that a miracle might occur and we might not know that it has. This is different from the claim that an event's being a miracle is independent of our epistemic state. Hume is drawing our attention to the fact that there could be an event which violates a well-confirmed lawlike statement yet remains unknown to us— for instance, a feather's going from rest to motion despite an unrecognized absence of any force acting on it.

Thus, there is ample evidence to take Hume's conception of a miracle to be that of an event that violates a well-confirmed lawlike

behaviour" (*An Enquiry Concerning Human Understanding* [student edition], p. 45). On its surface, this construal leaves it mysterious why the marvelous, the miraculous, and the probability of testimony should be related as Hume's remarks suggest.

12. "Of Miracles," note 23 (this is the third footnote of "Of Miracles").

statement: his criterion for application of the term; his talk of an event's *becoming miraculous* and of one event's *being more miraculous than* another; the way in which he relates marvelous events to miraculous ones; and most importantly, his general movement from an event's being a miracle to the strength of evidence against it, and hence against the correctness of testimony on the event's behalf. As will soon be clear, the entire structure of his argument depends on this movement, so we risk a complete failure of understanding if we interpret "miracle" in such a way as to make that transition problematic.

1.2.   Before turning to Hume's argument, we need to address two questions that this construal of "miracle" raises. First, does it not directly flout what Hume actually says? For as we saw, he writes several times that a miracle is a violation of the laws of nature. But does this signal a tension or even a confusion within Hume, or is it rather a tip-off about how best to understand his claim that a statement is a law of nature? Hume is frequently keen on having us attend to the conditions under which we apply a term or make a judgment. And there is a verificationistic streak in his thinking that often moves him to insist that there is nothing more to the content of the judgment in question beyond the thought that those conditions hold; this approach manifests itself on a number of occasions in the *Enquiry*. Now for Hume, we judge that some statement reports a causal regularity—that is, is a law of nature—under quite specific kinds of circumstances. We judge that "For all x, if Fx then Gx" is a law when our experience provides us with evidence that "Fx and Gx" holds for many values of x while failing to provide us with evidence that "Fx and not-Gx" holds for any value of x. Though I shall not press the point here, it is plausible to read Hume as saying that this is in fact part of *what we mean* when we judge a description to be a law.

If Hume does operate with something like this construal of natural law, then there need be no conflict in what he says about miracles: to say that an event has violated a law would just be to say that it has violated a statement for which we have a considerable degree of evidence. Of course, on this understanding, it makes sense to judge that a law of nature has been violated. But as we shall see, this is a desired result in this context because Hume *does* believe that one can imagine circumstances in which one would be justified in judging that a miracle had occurred.[13]

Second, we must ask how much evidence is required for us to claim that a general statement is a law of nature—that is, given Hume's characterization, how strong must the evidence be against an event for it to qualify as a miracle? For Hume, laws just are lawlike statements for which our evidence rises to the level of what he calls "proof." Consider what Hume says here, in a passage already partially quoted:

> There must, therefore, be a uniform experience against every miraculous event, otherwise the event would not merit that appellation. And as a uniform experience amounts to a proof, there is here a direct and full *proof,* from the nature of the fact, against the existence of any miracle.[14]

The evidence against a miracle is just the evidence in favor of the confirmed lawlike claim with which it conflicts. Because, according to Hume, the evidence against a miracle is a uniform experience that amounts to a proof, so too must be the evidence in favor of the lawlike claim with which the miracle conflicts.

This passage also makes clear that by "proof" Hume does not mean a demonstrative argument. A proof consists of a "uniform experience," one that is "firm and unalterable."[15] How uniform and firm? Hume tells us:

> Mr. Locke divides all arguments into demonstrative and probable. In this view, we must say, that it is only probable all men must die, or that the sun will rise to-morrow. But to conform our language more to common use, we ought to divide arguments into *demonstrations, proofs,* and *probabilities.* By *proofs* meaning such arguments from experience as leave no room for doubt or opposition.[16]

We judge a claim to be a law of nature only when we take the evidence to support it beyond the shadow of a doubt.

---

13. This point is not always appreciated, and I shall turn to it later.
14. "Of Miracles," paragraph 12.
15. "Of Miracles," paragraph 12.
16. *An Enquiry Concerning Human Understanding,* Section 6, note 10 (this is the first footnote of "Of Probability").

It is important to keep this in mind, that a proof consists of empirical evidence of a very high order. For otherwise, recalling that a miracle is a violation of a law of nature—that is, a transgression of a lawlike statement for which we have a proof—one might again be tempted to interpret Hume as making an *a priori* argument against miracles. Rather, what we have arrived at is a more accurate characterization of what he takes miracles to be—namely, events that violate a lawlike claim that our observations leave beyond doubt. What is analytic, if you will, is that a miracle claim confronts experiences that "leave no room" to accept its truth. By the nature of the case, there is much to be said for not crediting such a claim. But this is not in serious dispute since most people would agree that, amongst the total evidence, there are extraordinarily good reasons for not believing that a miraculous event has occurred: such an event is alleged to be a *miracle* after all. Nor does it settle the matter against rational belief in miracles, for as we shall soon see, Hume believes that a proof can be overwhelmed by a contrary proof.

2

HUME'S THEOREM

2.1.   Now that we have clarified Hume's working conception of a miracle, we can state:

> HUME'S THEOREM: It is not rational to believe on the basis of testimony that a miracle of a religious nature has occurred.[1]

At one point, Hume builds a connection to religion into the conception of a miracle: "A miracle may be accurately defined, *a transgression of a law of nature by a particular volition of the Deity, or by the interposition of some*

---

1. William Paley coined the nice phrase "Hume's Theorem" in 1794 in his *A View of the Evidences of Christianity,* James Miller, 1860, p. 16. Though its use risks the misinterpretation that Hume's argument is *a priori*, the phrase is too good to leave behind.

invisible agent."[2] If we do so, then Hume's Theorem can be simplified to: It is not rational to believe on the basis of testimony that a miracle has occurred. Because Hume thinks, despite this last gloss, that there could be miracles of a nonreligious nature, I find it preferable to adhere to the original, less streamlined formulation of Hume's Theorem.

Hume's Theorem can be made vivid by imagining Hume presenting himself with the following thought experiment: *I have many beliefs about the natural world, including the doings of my fellow humans. These beliefs are largely justifiable on the basis of my experience. Some of these beliefs are far more strongly justified than others. Some are so justified as to leave no room for doubt. Now, imagine that someone tells me one such belief is false (where this falsity is of some religious significance). For instance, imagine someone tells me that he saw a man raise someone from the dead. Or that he saw a man control the motion of the Moon. Would it be rational for me, on the basis of this testimony or any number of such testimonials, to reject my belief that the dead remain dead or that humans cannot will celestial bodies to do their bidding?* Hume's Theorem is his answer. Hume believed he had an argument, an "everlasting check" that rational individuals in this position could rehearse for themselves, to show that the answer is No.[3]

There has been scholarly dispute over where in Section 10 of the *Enquiry* Hume takes himself to have established his result. Many believe that Hume's argument is essentially over by the end of Part 1.[4] This

---

2. "Of Miracles," in *An Enquiry Concerning Human Understanding* (critical edition), Tom L. Beauchamp (editor), Oxford, 2006, pp. 83–99; note 23 (this is the third footnote of "Of Miracles"). Kemp Smith and others think that this version of Hume's definition reveals his conception of miracles as events that are supernaturally caused. I argued in footnote 2 of Chapter 1 that this is incorrect. Hume's reference here to religion is indeed important, but not because it helps us to locate his conception of a miracle; I shall turn to this below.

3. "Of Miracles," paragraph 2.

4. Don Garrett sums up the prevailing practice (in which he participates) when he writes that "commentators sometimes refer to the argument of Part i as Hume's '*a priori* argument' concerning miracles, and to the four arguments of Part ii as his '*a posteriori* arguments'" (*Cognition and Commitment in Hume's Philosophy,* Oxford, 1997, p. 137). This approach—seeing Hume's essay as offering both *a priori* and *a posteriori* arguments against belief in miracles—is explicitly defended (unsuccessfully, to my mind) by Robert A. Larmer in his "Interpreting Hume on Miracles," *Religious Studies,* vol. 45, 2009, pp. 325–38.

The practice easily leads to confusions or, at the very least, to confusing expositions. For instance, in J. C. A. Gaskin's analysis of Hume's "*a priori* argument," he writes:

> The veracity of human testimony is, from experience, normally a strong probability and as such amounts to a proof that what is reported took place. But sometimes the veracity of human testimony is a weak probability (as is always the case, according to Hume's

raises the awkward question of why Hume does not end "Of Miracles" right there but instead goes on for twice as long again in Part 2. Even more awkward for this reading is the fact that Hume's explicit summary of his conclusion at the end of Part 1 is *not* Hume's Theorem. There, he sums up his foregoing discussion by articulating "a general maxim worthy of our attention":

> That no testimony is sufficient to establish a miracle, unless the testimony be of such a kind, that its falsehood would be more miraculous, than the fact, which it endeavours to establish. And even in that case, there is a mutual destruction of arguments, and the superior only gives us an assurance suitable to that degree of force, which remains, after deducting the inferior.[5]

If we examine this first maxim, we do not find an unconditional claim of the form of Hume's Theorem. The first, and governing, sentence is all but explicitly a conditional claim (since we understand "*p* unless *q*" to mean "if not-*q*, then *p*"). It is logically equivalent to the following:

> FIRST LEMMA: If the falsehood of testimony on behalf of an alleged miraculous event is not "more miraculous" than the event itself, then it is not rational to believe in the occurrence of that event on the basis of that testimony.

---

arguments in Part 2, with reports of miracles). *Therefore*, from 3 and 4, when testimony is given which is contrary to our invariable experience, a probability, whether weak or strong, is opposing a certainty and (from 1 and 2) the wise man will believe the certainty. ("Hume on Religion," in *The Cambridge Companion to Hume,* David Fate Norton [editor], Cambridge, 1993, pp. 313–44; pp. 329–30.) The conclusion of this argument—that a wise man ought never to believe testimony on behalf of miracles over a certainty—follows only because we are appealing to empirical considerations (of the kind Hume discusses in Part 2, as Gaskin notes in his parenthetical remark). Hence, the argument cannot be *a priori*. (Gaskin's exposition is also confusing because the last quoted sentence suggests that a certainty always defeats "a probability, whether weak or strong." And yet the first sentence suggests that a strong probability "as such amounts to a proof." But if by "certainty" Gaskin means a claim for which we have a proof, then it is by no means given ahead of time which proof, if either, will carry the day.)

One exception to this unhappy practice is Robert J. Fogelin's analysis in his *A Defense of Hume on Miracles,* Princeton, 2003.

5. "Of Miracles," paragraph 13.

This says that if the evidence that speaks to the reliability of the testimony on behalf of the miraculous event is not greater than the evidence that speaks to the reliability of the claim with which that event conflicts, then it is not reasonable to believe the testimony. In other words, one must weigh the evidence in favor of the reliability of the kind of testimony one has on behalf of the miraculous event against the evidence in favor of the candidate law of nature that the miracle violates. It is not reasonable to believe in the miracle if the balance tilts toward the candidate law or is even level.

Hume does not, in Part 1 of his essay, discharge the antecedent of this conditional. As we shall see, that task is precisely the focus of Hume's discussion in Part 2. Since Hume's Theorem is in effect the consequent of this conditional, it is only established by taking Parts 1 and 2 together. We should view Hume's Theorem as the logical consequence of two lemmas, the first of which is established in Part 1 and the second in Part 2 of his essay.

It is correct, as far as it goes, to say that Hume's task in Part 1 is to argue for the First Lemma. But the deeper observation is that his goal there is to make the claim *intelligible*. Hume's First Lemma articulates a sufficient condition for the irrationality of belief in a miracle based on testimony—but what, precisely, is the content of this condition? Hume must have considered it an important philosophical contribution simply to have elucidated its substance. A major function of Part 1, in fact, is to provide a philosophical analysis that will answer this question and so allow untroubled appeal to the First Lemma.

To see how a doubt about this might arise, let us consider the following claim: *Obama was born within the rings of Saturn.* Under what conditions would a judicious person believe this claim? He will, Hume might say, weigh the pros and cons. The cons here simply consist in the highly warranted statements with which this claim conflicts—for instance, that humans have never ventured close to Saturn. I am extraordinarily confident that no one has ever done so, and that belief is simply at odds with the claim that Obama was born within Saturn's rings. This confidence is of course based on my experiences, on everything that I have observed about the world to date. Now, what are the pros in the case of this claim? Let us imagine that the pros consist solely of someone's telling me that Obama was born within the rings of Saturn. To arrive at a judgment regarding the claim, I must weigh this evidence and this counterevidence against one another. But how? On the face of it, they appear quite incommensurable: on the one hand, we have particular experiences and, on the other, someone's testimony. How can these be compared?

Hume suggests that we can only make progress here by offering an analysis of the rational force of testimony that renders such force commensurable with the experience that supports a candidate law of nature. His idea is that testimony's force itself derives from a candidate law of nature, one that links talk and truth. Just as what makes bear tracks evidentially relevant to the presence of bears is that we have good reason to believe that wherever there are bear tracks there will also be bears, so too a particular instance of testimony gets its evidential force from a well-supported correlation between someone's telling one that the world is a certain way and the world's actually being that way. Someone's saying that there is a tiger around the corner and there being a tiger around the corner are two distinct states of affairs in the natural world; however, the first can give us grounds for expecting the second if we have reason to believe that events of the first kind are reliably correlated with events of the second. The claim that testimony and world are correlated is a claim fully on a par with any other about the natural world; it is a perfectly respectable candidate for being a law of nature. Thus, the degree of warrant that one attaches to this presumptive law is transferred to the claim that Obama was born within the rings of Saturn via someone's telling one that Obama was born within the rings of Saturn.

In what coin can one measure this warrant, and how much is it worth? If we have good reason to believe that a correlation exists between testimony and truth, it is solely on the basis of experience. If this correlation has considerable warrant for us, this must consist in a wealth of experiences that confirm the claim. And Hume would insist that, in general, it does have considerable warrant: events of these different kinds (viz., reports that the world is so and the world's being so) are not capriciously related to one another. In general, our experiences strongly support the claim that what people tell us turns out to be true.

So, at the root of our confidence in testimony lies the same basis that grounds our confidence in any natural regularity. "It is experience only," Hume says, "which gives authority to human testimony; and it is the same experience, which assures us of the laws of nature."[6] The critical upshot is that the very same kind of evidence speaking in favor of the regularity that would be violated by Obama's having been born within the rings of Saturn also speaks in favor of the regularity that would be violated by Obama's not having been born within the rings of Saturn. Hume has rendered the evidence in favor of the event and that against it commensurable.

Given this achievement, it now makes sense to weigh the evidence in favor of Obama's having been born within the rings of Saturn against the evidence opposed to it. For Hume, this weighing is effected, at least metaphorically, by placing the evidence in favor in one pan of a balance scale and that opposed in the other. It is rational, he insists, to believe a claim insofar as the evidence for it outweighs the evidence against it, and in that case, the strength of one's conviction is determined by the extent to which the evidence in favor outweighs the evidence against. As Hume puts it, we have here "a contest of two opposite experiences; of which the one destroys the other, as far as its force goes, and the superior can only operate on the mind by the force, which remains."[7]

We can now return to the argument for the First Lemma, restated here:

> FIRST LEMMA: If the falsehood of testimony on behalf of an alleged miraculous event is not "more miraculous" than the event itself, then it is not rational to believe in the occurrence of that event on the basis of that testimony.

We shall argue for this lemma by assuming its antecedent to be true and deriving its consequent. So, we assume that the falsehood of testimony on behalf of some miraculous event e is not "more miraculous" than e itself. Recall that to say one event is more miraculous than another is to say that the evidence in favor of the lawlike claim with which the first event conflicts is stronger than the evidence in favor of the lawlike claim with which the second event conflicts. Given Hume's central

---

6. "Of Miracles," paragraph 35. The point is repeated elsewhere in "Of Miracles" in very similar words: "The very same principle of experience, which gives us a certain degree of assurance in the testimony of witnesses, gives us also, in this case, another degree of assurance against the fact, which they endeavour to establish" (paragraph 8). Hume first touches on this central observation in paragraph 5.

7. "Of Miracles," paragraph 8.

commensurating analysis in Part 1 of his essay, it is indeed meaningful to evaluate whether the relation *is a greater miracle than* holds between an event's occurrence and a testimony's falsehood (because we can now appreciate that there is a lawlike claim about nature with which the falsehood of that testimony conflicts). From our assumption, then, it follows that the evidence in favor of the lawlike claim that testimony is reliable is not greater than the evidence in favor of the lawlike claim with which *e* conflicts. But evidence in favor of the lawlike claim that testimony is reliable is precisely evidence in favor of *e*'s having occurred. And evidence in favor of the lawlike claim with which *e* conflicts is just evidence against *e*'s having occurred. So, the evidence in favor of *e*'s having occurred is not greater than the evidence against *e*'s having occurred. Hence, belief in *e*'s having occurred would have either no warrant or negative warrant. It is not rational to believe a claim under those circumstances. Therefore, it is not rational to believe that *e* occurred. This is the consequent of the First Lemma. After discharging our assumption, we arrive at the conditional claim that is the First Lemma itself, which is thereby established.

Some observations are in order here. First, to repeat, the First Lemma is the upshot of Part 1 of Hume's essay. He does not, in Part 1, assess the strength of the lawlike claim regarding the reliability of testimony (especially testimony on behalf of miracles deemed to be of religious significance), an assessment that would be required in order to pass judgment on the First Lemma's antecedent. Consequently, Hume is not yet in a position to assert the consequent of the First Lemma—that is, Hume's Theorem. And indeed, nowhere there does he assert it. It is a mistake to think that Hume's argument against miracles is concluded by the end of Part 1.

Second, and an observation about Hume's discussion in Part 1 that cannot be too often repeated, while the argument for the First Lemma is clearly of importance, what is of greater philosophical interest is Hume's thought that he needed to make the Lemma *intelligible* in the first place. Hume's argument in Part 1 for the First Lemma is comparatively brief: it is really the focus of just one (the final) paragraph.[8] Most of the remainder of Part 1 is taken up with a discussion of testimony intended to provide an analysis according to which the evidence for a miraculous event's occurrence and the evidence against its occurrence

---

8. "Of Miracles," paragraph 13.

are after all commensurable. Since Hume had already announced that all regularities concerning matters of fact require justification by experience (and in that respect are commensurable), the philosophically crucial step in Part 1 is Hume's conception of how testimony fits into the economy of rational belief via a natural regularity between word and world, which an individual's testimony partially instances. Hume surely thought that his conception marked an advance, not least in allowing one to interpret a previously obscure question, about the rationality of belief in miracles on the basis of testimony, in such a way that it turned on intelligible and straightforward considerations—namely, the comparison of evidence for lawlike claims.

An advance on whom, however? Most notably and immediately, an advance on John Locke. For he observed that a problem confronts us when we are in possession of both sensory evidence and conflicting testimonial evidence: in such circumstances, where ought we to incline our assent? "The difficulty," Locke writes, "is, when Testimonies contradict common experience, and the reports of History and Witnesses clash with the ordinary course of nature, or with one another." Locke, like Hume, embraces the image of our subsequently needing to balance the strength of these competing considerations, "nicely weighing every particular Circumstance," he says. But the true "difficulty" for Locke is that he guts the metaphor of weighing of all significance because he goes on to claim that neither of these two competing considerations is reducible to the other: there are, he says, "two foundations of Credibility, *viz.* Common Observation in like cases, and particular Testimonies in that particular instance."[9] If these are really two distinct foundations, how are they to be weighed against one another, and what sense does such a weighing even have? Hume felt the problem and proposed a solution: there is only one foundation of credibility, for the evidential strength of testimony ultimately depends on common observation.

Third, and related to the second observation above, this was a philosophical innovation that simply passed some of Hume's critics by. For instance, George Campbell, in his *A Dissertation on Miracles* (1762), expresses the following concern about Hume's discussion:

---

9. John Locke, *An Essay Concerning Human Understanding*, Peter H. Nidditch (editor), Oxford, 1975, Book IV, Chapter XVI, Section 9, p. 663.

There is in *arithmetic* a rule called REDUCTION, by which numbers of different denominations are brought to the same denomination. If this ingenious author shall invent a rule in *logic* analogous to this, for reducing different classes of evidence to the same class, he will bless the world with a most important discovery. . . . But till this metaphysical *reduction* be discovered, it will be impossible, where the evidences are of different orders, to ascertain by *subtraction* the superior evidence.

Campbell charges that the evidences at issue are "heterogeneal" and that, in the light of this, talk of balancing the arguments in favor of a miracle against those opposed to it are of "little significancy."[10] However, this way of putting the matter suggests that he has missed the fact that a central philosophical point of Part 1 is precisely the provision of a conception of testimonial evidence that makes room for such a "reduction." One may find this conception unsatisfactory, but one should not fail to acknowledge its existence and the philosophical work to which Hume puts it in "Of Miracles."

Fourth, it is important not to read the First Lemma in such a way that it is a truism. We can turn to Campbell again for an early instance of this, for this was no doubt the reading he had in mind when he charged that the upshot of Hume's discussion in Part 1 "contains a most certain truth, though at the same time the least significant, that ever perhaps was ushered into the world with so much solemnity."[11] On this reading, Hume advises us not to believe in the occurrence of an allegedly miraculous event if the probability of its occurrence is not greater than the probability of its nonoccurrence, which is "a most certain truth" indeed. But what Hume asks us to compare is the probability that a certain kind of testimony is reliable and the probability that a lawlike statement will hold. Our judgment about the event's occurrence, Hume says, should be sensitive to our weighing of the evidence in favor of the reliability of a certain kind of testimony against

---

10. George Campbell's *A Dissertation on Miracles* (originally published in 1762), reprinted in *Early Responses to Hume,* Volume 6 (second edition, revised), James Fieser (editor), Thoemmes, 2005, pp. 1–114; pp. 27–28.

11. Campbell, *A Dissertation on Miracles,* pp. 52–53.

the evidence in favor of a particular lawlike claim. If we could not assess the evidence for a certain kind of testimony's being reliable independently of the evidence for the event's occurrence, then we might find ourselves heading toward triviality. But we can, and so the threat of triviality dissipates.[12]

Finally, it is worth observing that the debate about miracles is just one application of Hume's conception of testimony and how it relates to rational belief. Another application of no less interest to Hume is to the general question of what makes historical inquiry possible, of how knowledge about the past can be acquired. Hume likens this knowledge to an extension of our experience:

> If we consider the shortness of human life, and our limited knowledge, even of what passes in our time, we must be sensible that we should be for ever children in understanding, were it not for this invention, which extends our experience to all past ages, and to the most distant nations; making them contribute as much to our improvement in wisdom, as if they had actually lain under our observation. A man acquainted with history may, in some respect, be said to have lived from the beginning of the world, and to have been making continual additions to his stock of knowledge in every century.[13]

But that history enables others' experiences to become one's own is a metaphor. Hume's conception, as elaborated in "Of Miracles," allows him to cash it in for a more readily intelligible claim. While we cannot have a historical figure's experiences, historical narrative allows us to have justified beliefs about the world that coincide with beliefs held by a historical individual on the basis of his or her experiences.

For instance, on the basis of his own observations, James Boswell concluded that Hume was in good spirits even as he neared death.

---

12. For some further discussion and references, see also Peter Millican's "Twenty Questions about Hume's 'Of Miracles'," in Anthony O'Hear (editor), *Philosophy and Religion,* Supplement of the Royal Institute of Philosophy, Cambridge, 2011, pp. 151–92; p. 164 and footnote 15. I disagree with Millican about what Hume needs to assume in order to avoid this triviality; for further discussion, see footnote 22 below.
13. "Of the Study of History," in *Essays: Moral, Political, and Literary,* pp. 563–68; pp. 566–67.

Boswell reported these conclusions in writing, which I and others can read. Nothing about Hume can be inferred by me from a bare encounter with these recollections: what does Hume's mental state in 1776 have to do with the words that one finds in a book printed this year? But if I also reflect that I have good grounds for believing that the world often is as it is reported to be, then it is rational for me too now to believe that Hume was in good spirits even as he neared death. "What would become of *history*," Hume asked, "had we not a dependence on the veracity of the historian, according to the experience, which we have had of mankind?"[14] Historical knowledge would be a mystery, Hume thought, were it not for the conception of human testimony that the first half of "Of Miracles" elaborates upon and defends. With it in place, our knowledge of the past is no more (or less) mysterious than our knowledge of physics. Our confidence that Hume faced death cheerfully is cut from the same cloth as our conviction that there will be a lunar eclipse on May 20, 2953.[15]

2.2.   Hume has now arrived at Part 2, having established just this:

> FIRST LEMMA: If the falsehood of testimony on behalf of an alleged miraculous event is not "more miraculous" than the event itself, then it is not rational to believe in the occurrence of that event on the basis of that testimony.

The central business of Part 2 is to establish the antecedent of the First Lemma:

> SECOND LEMMA: The falsehood of testimony on behalf of an alleged miraculous event of a religious nature is not "more miraculous" than the event itself.

From these two lemmas, Hume's Theorem immediately follows.

The Second Lemma is an empirical claim. Establishing it requires examination of the evidence in favor of the reliability of testimony in

---

14. "Of Liberty and Necessity," *An Enquiry Concerning Human Understanding*, Tom L. Beauchamp (editor), Oxford, 2006, Section 8, paragraph 18.

15. See http://eclipse.gsfc.nasa.gov/LEcat5/LE2901-3000.html, accessed July 1, 2015.

general and, more specifically, of testimony on behalf of events deemed to be of religious significance. This evidence then needs to be weighed against the evidence in favor of the lawlike claim with which the alleged event is in conflict. Hume is explicit in the very first paragraph of Part 2 that nothing he has written thus far assures us of the outcome of this weighing; for all we know, the evidence in favor of the reliability of testimony on behalf of a religiously significant miracle outweighs the evidence in favor of the lawlike claim with which this alleged event conflicts. But in fact, "it is easy to show," Hume then says, that this is not the case; this is the burden of Part 2 of his essay.[16]

The empirical nature of this inquiry is plain, and it shows that Hume's Theorem, though logically deducible from our two lemmas, is not justifiable *a priori*. Its justification ultimately depends on general facts about human psychology. Hume was likely aware of this possible misinterpretation, for we find him correcting phrases that might suggest he was offering an *a priori* argument. For instance, in the first two editions of the *Enquiry*, he wrote that "no testimony for any kind of miracle *can ever possibly* amount to a probability, much less to a proof."[17] Hume amended this in the 1756 edition, however, and in all nine subsequent editions to pass through his hands, we read instead that "no testimony for any kind of miracle *has ever* amounted to a probability, much less to a proof."[18] His claims about testimony were intended to be understood not as reports on relations between ideas but rather as reports on matters of fact.

Hume distinguishes four points that speak to this conclusion. The first three are squarely psychological or historical in nature. His first observation is that our evidence for the reliability of testimony is strongest when the reports come from the mouths of many people who possess good sense, education, and integrity; who have reputations it would be painful for them to see tarnished; and who are testifying to an event that occurred in public and in such circumstances as to make detection of fraud an easy matter.[19] Hume states that throughout "all history," reports of miracles have failed to meet these conditions.

---

16. "Of Miracles," paragraph 14.
17. "Of Miracles," paragraph 35.
18. *An Enquiry Concerning Human Understanding* (critical edition), p. 262, emphasis added.
19. "Of Miracles," paragraph 15.

Hume's second observation is that people suffer from what he calls a *propensity to the marvelous*. In an insightful passage, he describes its nature and source:

> The passion of *surprize* and *wonder*, arising from miracles, being an agreeable emotion, gives a sensible tendency towards the belief of those events, from which it is derived. And this goes so far, that even those who cannot enjoy this pleasure immediately, nor can believe those miraculous events, of which they are informed, yet love to partake of the satisfaction at second-hand or by rebound, and place a pride and delight in exciting the admiration of others.[20]

People delight in the sensation of wonder that a belief in marvelous events induces. This fact is pertinent to the evaluation of evidence for the reliability of testimony for such events: the pleasurable sensation can even be enjoyed sympathetically, "by rebound," through beholding its primary effect on others, in addition to the pleasure one takes in being the cause of such esteemed sensations in others. The power of this propensity to the marvelous is effectively evidence against the trustworthiness of testimony on behalf of the marvelous.

When the marvels at issue are of a religious nature, Hume observes, additional psychological considerations potentiate our propensity to the marvelous. The feelings of self-importance, urgency, and fear that can attend the delivery of a message one deems to be of religious significance thoroughly overwhelm people's honesty and critical faculties:

> But what greater temptation than to appear a missionary, a prophet, an ambassador from heaven? Who would not encounter many dangers and difficulties, in order to attain so sublime a character? Or if, by the help of vanity and a heated imagination, a man has first made a convert of himself, and entered seriously into the delusion; who ever scruples to make use of pious frauds, in support of so holy and meritorious a cause?[21]

---

20. "Of Miracles," paragraph 16.
21. "Of Miracles," paragraph 29.

This potent cocktail of psychological dispositions, for which history and our own experience furnish us with ample evidence, makes it impossible to treat testimony on behalf of religious marvels as reliable: "if the spirit of religion join itself to the love of wonder, there is an end of common sense; and human testimony, in these circumstances, loses all pretensions to authority."[22]

Hume's third observation is of a historical nature and reinforces the first two. Most reports of miracles, Hume says, can be traced back to

---

22. "Of Miracles," paragraph 17.

Millican claims that Hume accepts what he calls the "Independence Assumption." According to this, "Different 'kinds' of testimony (specified in terms of the character and number of the witnesses, their consistency and manner of delivery, etc.) carry a different typical probability of truth and falsehood *independently of the event reported*" ("Twenty Questions about Hume's 'Of Miracles'," p. 164). Yet it is clear from Part 2 that Hume does not accept this: he treats the fact that some testimony is on behalf of an event deemed religiously significant to be a very pertinent fact indeed in evaluating the testimony's evidential heft. Even though it is clearly something that Hume rejects, much of Millican's discussion proceeds as if this assumption is properly attributed to him. Millican eventually acknowledges that Hume cannot after all be understood to embrace this assumption (pp. 184–85).

Millican is led to impute this to Hume for several reasons. First, he believes it is demanded by what Hume says, especially when the latter writes of considering the evidential weight of "the testimony, considered apart and in itself" and of its weight when taken as "testimony . . . of such a kind" ("Of Miracles," paragraphs 11, 13). These snippets need not push us toward Millican's construal, however. When Hume asks us to consider the force of testimony "considered apart and in itself," the context suggests that he means to ask us to ignore, temporarily, the downgrading of the evidential force of such testimony that must eventually result from considering all the proof-like evidence in favor of the natural regularity with which the alleged miraculous event conflicts. Bracketing such counterevidence, Hume says, just might leave us with testimony whose evidence amounts to a proof, and we would then ultimately be faced with weighing "proof against proof" (paragraph 11). In sum, what Hume is considering the testimony apart from is not the kind of event it is testimony on behalf of but rather the evidence against the event testified to. Likewise, when Hume refers to testimony "of such a kind, that its falsehood would be more miraculous, than the fact, which it endeavours to establish" (paragraph 13), it is unclear why Millican thinks that, in characterizing this "kind," Hume will not want to make reference to the sorts of events on behalf of which the testimony speaks. Indeed, Hume goes on to argue that experience tells us one kind of testimony whose falsehood is not more miraculous than the event it testifies to is precisely testimony on behalf of miraculous events deemed to have religious significance. When Hume writes of "a kind" of testimony, in the context of evaluations of evidential significance, there is good reason to think that one individuating consideration in play is the kind of event the testimony is on behalf of. For instance, and most relevantly, testimonies on behalf of extraordinary events deemed to be of religious significance are not the testimony of "ignorant and barbarous" people.[23] These are not people whose testimony satisfies the conditions of reliability articulated in Hume's first observation. Furthermore, because education provides a partial check on our propensity to the marvelous (and perhaps also to religious enthusiasm), which otherwise exercises unbridled influence on the mind, the genesis of most miraculous tales in the reports of uneducated peoples must further incline us to discount their trustworthiness.

In sum, we do not have strong reasons to credit historical or contemporary reports of miracles; indeed, our experience provides us with reasons for being skeptical of such reports.[24] "Upon the whole, then," Hume summarizes the thrust of these psychological and historical observations, "it appears, that no testimony for any kind of miracle has ever amounted to a probability, much less to a proof."[25] He immediately reminds his reader that the considerations he has offered apply most

---

of the same kind, when it comes to evidential evaluation, as testimonies on behalf of mundane events.

Second, Millican worries that if we do not impute the Independence Assumption to Hume, then the upshot of Part 1 of his essay turns into a truism ("Twenty Questions about Hume's 'Of Miracles'," p. 164). He believes that if Hume does not hold the Independence Assumption, then he cannot "identify 'kinds' of testimony, with their own typical probability of truth and falsehood" (and that if he cannot do this, then the threat of vacuity looms; p. 164). But this seems incorrect. As just noted, Hume can reject the Independence Assumption and still speak of kinds of testimony, where now one kind-individuating factor is the kind of event the testimony is on behalf of.

23. "Of Miracles," paragraph 20.

24. That this is Hume's position continues to elude commentators. For instance, J. Houston says:

> Hume's own view that having an improbable content in itself counts against the report's probability *would* be justified as a conclusion of such an empirical enquiry, if indeed experience were to reveal a correlation between a report's having an improbable content, and that report's being found to be false. However, Hume seems to have thought his view to be self-evident and did not attempt this sort of necessary empirical justification. (*Reported Miracles*, Cambridge, 1994, p. 153.)

It is one thing to think that Hume's arguments are not compelling, but quite another to believe that he has offered no arguments at all. Part 2 of Hume's essay is precisely an attempt to sketch the empirical considerations about human psychology that lead him to judge that little stock should be placed in the reliability of testimony on behalf of extraordinary events deemed to be of religious significance.

25. "Of Miracles," paragraph 35.

strongly when the miracle is of a religious nature: "I beg the limitations here made be remarked, when I say, that a miracle can never be proved, so as to be the foundation of a system of religion."[26] The falsity of testimony on behalf of a miraculous event of religious significance would conflict with no proven, or even minimally confirmed, lawlike statement.

Again, it is important to appreciate that Hume is not saying testimony necessarily falls short of a proof of a miracle. If this were his position, then his working definition of "miracle"—in effect, an event against whose occurrence experience has furnished us with a proof—would simply entail that testimony could not possibly make it rational to believe that a miracle had occurred, or even to withhold judgment about whether it had.

For Hume, there is no contradiction in supposing testimony to furnish us with a proof of a miracle that overwhelms the evidence against the miracle. He sees no inconsistency in supposing "that the testimony, considered apart and in itself, amounts to an entire proof,"[27] or in other words, in supposing that "there may possibly be miracles, or violations of the usual course of nature, of such a kind as to admit of proof from human testimony."[28] As a matter of fact, this has not happened: "it will be impossible," he suggests, "to find any such in all the records of history."[29] But that does not make it impossible *tout court*. There is no contradiction in supposing that a miracle "comes within the reach of human testimony."[30]

By way of example, Hume points out that testimony could in principle make it "certain" that "from the first of January 1600, there was a total darkness over the whole earth for eight days."[31] This example is present in the very first edition of the *Enquiry* and in each of the ten subsequent editions prepared by Hume. Originally, however, it appeared only in a footnote. In the last three editions, beginning in 1770, Hume moved the discussion into the body of the text itself.[32] Perhaps Hume had encountered one misinterpretation too many and was determined

---

26. "Of Miracles," paragraph 36.
27. "Of Miracles," paragraph 11.
28. "Of Miracles," paragraph 36.
29. "Of Miracles," paragraph 36.
30. "Of Miracles," paragraph 36.
31. "Of Miracles," paragraph 36.
32. See *An Enquiry Concerning Human Understanding* (critical edition), p. 262.

to make clear that his point about testimony was not definitional. Of course, it does not follow that Hume thought convincing testimony on behalf of such a celestial event was likely: if we keep in mind the considerations about human nature that Hume highlighted, such justifying testimony is not to be expected.

Even less likely is justifying testimony for another miraculous event that Hume considers: the resurrection of Queen Elizabeth I. Testimony here should count for even less, for the miracle concerns matters of substantial human interest, such as the lives of great personages and the flow of political power, which therefore have an even greater tendency to distort judgment. For Hume, "the knavery and folly of men are such common phenomena,"[33] especially as regards matters freighted with human significance, that it would be unreasonable to expect testimony ever to amount to a proof of the event.

Finally, when we turn to religious miracles, our experience gives us strong reason to deny supporting testimony any evidential weight at all, let alone the weight of proof. Everything we know about human nature—especially that, when it comes to religious matters, "there is an end of common sense"—makes it very reasonable not to credit such testimony at all. Thus if we were to learn that our informants take Elizabeth's resurrection (or eight days of darkness, or what have you) to be a part of a "new system of religion," then "this very circumstance would be a full proof of a cheat, and sufficient with all men of sense, not only to make them reject the fact, but even reject it without farther examination."[34] All "men of sense" realize that such testimony is of no evidential value and should count for nothing in the eventual weighing of the evidence for and against the event in question.

We can now understand better why Hume refers to deities in one of his elucidations of the concept *miracle*.[35] He does not intend, as some readers have supposed, to make the notion of divine causation part of the concept *miracle*. Rather, he does so to specify which miraculous events fall most squarely within the scope of his central thesis. The proper point of application of the notion of the supernatural is not to the kind of causation that brings about the event in question but rather

---

33. "Of Miracles," paragraph 37.
34. "Of Miracles," paragraph 38.
35. See footnote 2 above.

to the psychological state of those testifying to the event. For it is in those situations in which testimony is surrounded by religious concerns that experience informs us that the testimony provides no proof of the event it relates—indeed, that it provides no confirmation of its occurrence at all.

In sharp contrast to the fact that the unreliability of testimony on behalf of a religious miracle would conflict with no well-confirmed lawlike claim, let alone a proven one, the truth of such testimony would, by definition, conflict with a lawlike statement of which we have a proof. Recall that this is simply how Hume uses the term *miracle*. It is clear, then, that the testimonial evidence in favor of a miracle of a religious nature is far weaker than the evidence in favor of the lawlike claim with which the alleged miraculous event conflicts. Hence, the falsehood of testimony on behalf of an alleged miraculous event of a religious nature is not "more miraculous" than the event itself. This is precisely the Second Lemma.

Hume draws the obvious consequence from this and his First Lemma: a person's disposition to believe on the basis of testimony in miraculous occurrences of religious import, Hume says in the final words of his essay, "subverts all principles of his understanding, and gives him a determination to believe what is most contrary to custom and experience."[36] In sum, Hume's Theorem: it is not rational to believe on the basis of testimony that a miracle of a religious nature has occurred.

The bare statement of Hume's Theorem leaves open the possibility that, while it might not be rational to move from testimony on behalf of religious miracles to belief, such testimony should cause one to adjust one's confidence in the lawlike regularities with which the alleged miracles conflict. But in fact, if one recalls the elements of the proof of Hume's Theorem that we have just surveyed, it is plain that a far stronger conclusion is supported. On the basis of our experience of human psychology and behavior, Hume says, we should form "a general resolution, never to lend any attention to [testimony concerning religious miracles], with whatever specious pretense it may be covered."[37] Such testimony counts for nothing and so should occasion no revision of one's confidence in the natural regularities with which the alleged miracle conflicts.

---

36. "Of Miracles," paragraph 41.
37. "Of Miracles," paragraph 38.

3

HUME AND SELF-UNDERMINING

3.1. If this analysis of "Of Miracles" is accurate to this point, then it reveals Hume's exposition to be tighter than many of his interpreters have suspected and his argument to be more interesting and powerful than many of his critics have supposed. But we can take the analysis further by turning now to the opening words of Hume's essay, which have proved a challenge to many readers. In his very first sentence, Hume invokes John Tillotson (1630–94), who served as Archbishop of Canterbury, and attributes an argument to Tillotson against the "real presence"—that is, the Roman Catholic conviction that during Holy Communion the substance of the wine and of the wafer become that of the blood and of the body of Christ. Hume judges the argument to be "decisive" and tells us that he has "discovered an argument of a like nature" that applies more generally "to all kinds of superstitious delusions."[1] He then begins the exposition of the argument we have been considering until now.

Hume's comments on Tillotson are very instructive because they lead to two interpretive checks: we must show, first, that Tillotson's argument as Hume summarizes it coincides with Hume's argument as we have understood it and, second, that Tillotson's argument in fact resembles Hume's summary of it. A failure in the first task suggests a failure in our understanding of Hume's own argument; a failure in the second forces one to view Hume's invocation of Tillotson as either confused or overly mischievous. In meeting both challenges, we shall be led to an interesting perspective on Hume's argument.

So, what does Hume say about Tillotson? The latter, Hume tells us, offers the following claims: (1) the ultimate evidence for miracles consists of the direct observations of the original eyewitnesses; (2) the evidence provided by the testimony of these eyewitnesses is weaker than that provided to anyone by his or her direct observation; hence, (3) our evidence for the truth of the Christian miracle of the real presence is weaker than the evidence we have for claims we can now directly observe to be true; (4) we can now directly observe that this wine is not blood—that is, that the miracle of the real presence has not taken place; hence, (5) our evidence for the truth of the miracle of the real presence is weaker than our evidence against it; therefore, since "a weaker evidence can never destroy a stronger," (6) it is not rational for us now to believe that the Christian miracle of the real presence has taken place.[2]

Some scholars have drawn attention to elements of this argument that are foreign to Hume's treatment of miracles and wondered how much Tillotson, so understood, tells us about Hume.[3] For instance, claim 2—in effect, that testimony degrades the evidential strength of direct observation—does not play a role in Hume's own argument. Nevertheless, the structure of this argument is closely related to the core of Hume's. Schematically, Hume presents Tillotson's argument as involving a weighing of the evidence for and against the miracle claim. The evidence in favor consists of testimony, and the evidence against consists of direct observation. To guarantee that the two kinds of

1. "Of Miracles," "in *An Enquiry Concerning Human Understanding* (critical edition), Tom L. Beauchamp (editor), Oxford, 2006, pp. 83–99; paragraph 2.

2. "Of Miracles," paragraph 1.

3. See, for instance, Robert J. Fogelin, *A Defense of Hume on Miracles,* Princeton, 2003, p. 64.

evidence are commensurable and to reveal the result of their comparison is precisely the job of claim 2: its import is that direct observation provides weightier evidence than does testimony. Now, Hume's own argument proceeds very similarly, except that it does not help itself to a commensurating assumption but rather seeks to establish it. That the evidence against a miracle and the testimonial evidence for it are commensurable is the burden of Part 1 in "Of Miracles." And that the evidence against a miracle, especially one of a religious nature, is stronger than the evidence in its favor is argued for at length in Part 2. Thus, we can see how Tillotson's argument, as Hume presents it, provides a prototype for his own.

It is less clear how Hume's sketch of Tillotson's argument relates to what Tillotson intended. Again, some commentators have found little relation.[4] If we turn to Tillotson, we see that he offers several kinds of considerations against the miracle of transubstantiation.[5] Many of these are scripturally based, but one has a distinctly philosophical cast. He makes the point a number of different ways, but the following give a good sense of Tillotson's philosophical argument against transubstantiation:

> [B]y what clearer evidence or stronger Argument could any
> man prove to me that such words [supporting Transub-
> stantiation] were in the Bible, than I can prove to him that
> bread and wine after consecration are bread and wine still?
> He could but appeal to my eyes to prove such words to be in
> the Bible, and with the same reason and justice might I

4. Fogelin, for instance, concludes that "Hume's invocation of Tillotson is either overblown or ironic" (*A Defense of Hume on Miracles,* p. 66). David Wootton writes that "Hume gives only a careless account of Tillotson's argument" and that "Hume's argument is essentially different in character from Tillotson's" ("Hume's 'Of Miracles': Probability and Irreligion," in *Studies in the Philosophy of the Scottish Enlightenment,* M. A. Stewart [editor], Oxford, 1990, pp. 191–229; p. 207). Michael P. Levine argues that "Tillotson's argument against transubstantiation is very different than the argument Hume presents as Tillotson's" (*Hume and the Problem of Miracles: A Solution,* Kluwer, 1989, p. 135). Such reactions date almost from the publication of Hume's essay. For instance, George Campbell in 1762 wrote that Hume's "argument against *miracles* has not the least affinity to the argument used by Dr. Tillotson against *transubstantiation*" (*A Dissertation on Miracles,* reprinted in *Early Responses to Hume,* Volume 6 [second edition, revised], James Fieser [editor], Thoemmes, 2005, pp. 1–114; p. 30).
5. For one of Tillotson's most extended attacks, see his "Sermon XXVI: A Discourse against Transubstantiation," reprinted in his *Works* (second edition), printed by B. Aylmer and W. Rogers, London, 1699, pp. 297–317.

appeal to several of his senses to prove to him that the bread and wine after consecration are bread and wine still. . . .

Whether it be reasonable to manage that God should make that a part of the Christian Religion which shakes the main external evidence and confirmation of the whole? I mean the Miracles which were wrought by our Saviour and his Apostles, the assurance whereof did at first depend upon the certainty of sense. . . . Suppose then *Transubstantiation* to be part of the Christian Doctrine, it must have the same confirmation with the whole, and that is Miracles: But of all Doctrines in the world it is peculiarly incapable of being proved by a Miracle. For if a Miracle were wrought for the proof of it, the very same assurance which any man hath of the truth of the Miracle he hath of the falsehood of the Doctrine, that is the clear evidence of his Senses. . . . Transubstantiation is not to be proved by a Miracle, because that would be, *to prove to a Man by something that he sees, that he doth not see what he sees.*

[Transubstantiation] cannot be true unless our Senses, and the Senses of all mankind be deceived about their proper objects; and if this be true and certain, then nothing else can be so; for if we be not certain of what we see, we can be certain of nothing.[6]

These passages are open to the following reading. Our evidence for the miracle of transubstantiation ultimately depends on sense perception: either one witnesses directly a miracle that speaks in its favor, or one learns about such a miracle from others. But if the miracle of transubstantiation has just taken place, then what now appears in every respect to be bread is in fact not; that is, one's senses are quite capable of playing one false. Indeed, we appreciate that they can do so in such a gross fashion that our confidence is undercut that neither we nor those on whom we rely were deceived in what was seen. To contrapose Tillotson's formulation, the very same assurance one has of the truth of the doctrine one also has of the falsehood of the miracle—that is, of the unreliability of the evidence for it. The belief in transubstantiation

---

6. Tillotson, "Sermon XXVI: A Discourse against Transubstantiation," pp. 314–15.

is epistemically *self-undermining*: reflection on the belief undercuts one's grounds for holding it to be true. There is something unstable about one's epistemic position if one finds oneself believing such a self-undermining proposition. As Tillotson puts it, "And what can be more vain than to pretend, that a man may be assured that such a Doctrine is revealed by God, and consequently true, which if it be true, a man can have no assurance at all of any Divine Revelation?"[7] How can we believe a doctrine whose very truth undercuts our grounds for believing it?[8]

Whether the doctrine of transubstantiation succumbs to precisely this argument is not my concern. I am rather more interested in the style of argument that Tillotson here suggests. What Tillotson draws our attention to is the interesting fact that some claims can be evidentially self-undermining. To take them seriously undercuts the very evidence we have for taking them seriously. They are not "Liar sentences," for taking them to be true does not lead to the conclusion that they are false. They are rather epistemological cousins: taking such claims to be true leads to the conclusion that we lack grounds for holding them to be true. In its boldest form, such a sentence might simply assert that it is unjustifiable (as the Gödel sentence can be viewed as doing). But neither self-reference nor explicit mention of justification is essential. A claim about the world might, in conjunction with other beliefs held, lead someone to conclude that he or she could not after all be justified in believing the claim. For instance, "My memory is not reliable for events that occurred more than five seconds ago" may be such a claim. Given that taking in evidence about one's memory typically requires more than five seconds, my believing this claim should lead me to distrust any evidence I might be given for its correctness.

Such evidentially self-undermining claims also bear a family resemblance to the "norms of description" that so fascinated Wittgenstein in

---

7. Tillotson, "The Rule of Faith," reprinted in *Works*, pp. 649–755; p. 736. He adds memorably: "It is a wonder that any man who considers the natural consequences of this *Doctrine* can be a Papist; unless he have attained to Mr. *Cressy's* pitch of *Learning*, who speaking of the difficult Arguments wherewith this Doctrine was pressed, says plainly, *I must answer freely and ingenuously, that I have not learned to answer such Arguments, but to despise them.*"
8. John Trenchard (1662–1723) expresses the same thought as Tillotson when he says that the miracles of the papists "destroy the evidence they appeal to." ("On Miracles," posthumously printed in his *Essays on Important Subjects*, A. Millar, London, 1755, pp. 1–21; p. 20.)

On Certainty.[9] There, he focused on propositions the doubting of which, he claimed, made little sense. They were not so much testable as part of the very apparatus of testing. To subject them to doubt involved pulling the rug out from under one's feet, for the considerations one might deploy to bring them into doubt would all be less firmly held than the propositions being doubted. Wittgenstein illustrates the point this way in a typically arresting passage:

> If a blind man were to ask me "Have you got two hands?" I
> should not make sure by looking. If I were to have any doubt
> of it, then I don't know why I should trust my eyes. For why
> shouldn't I test my *eyes* by looking to find out whether I see
> my two hands?[10]

Wittgenstein focuses on propositions that one could not doubt without thereby bringing into question the very grounds for one's doubt.[11] Tillotson's propositions are those that one could not come to believe without thereby bringing into question one's very grounds for belief.

Now, many readers have found this argument of Tillotson's to be quite alien to Hume's own argument and, therefore, to the argument that Hume imputes to Tillotson at the outset of "Of Miracles."[12] Hume's

---

9. *On Certainty*, G. E. M. Anscombe and G. H. von Wright (editors), Harper Torchbooks, 1972; §167.

10. *On Certainty*, §125.

11. *On Certainty*, §98. See also §§456, 506, 516, 558, 650.

12. One of the few attempts to understand how Tillotson's argument provides a model for Hume's own is undertaken by Dennis M. Ahern in his "Hume on the Evidential Impossibility of Miracles," printed in *Studies in Epistemology*, American Philosophical Quarterly Monograph Series, No. 9, Basil Blackwell, 1975, pp. 1–31. Ahern suggests that if, on Hume's view, we judge an event to be a miracle, then we shall straightaway have to withdraw that judgment because "the occurrence of the alleged miracle . . . disproves the relevant proposed laws of nature" (p. 26). This is true enough, and I shall return to the observation in another context below. But it will not do as an adequate analysis of how Tillotson's argument can be seen in Hume's own. For the self-undermining highlighted here is purely a consequence of Hume's definition of "miracle"; no mention has yet been made of testimony, of Hume's argument, or of Hume's main conclusion. (Of course, one might think, as many have, that Hume's argument involves no more than the drawing of a trivial consequence from his definition, but we have seen that this is quite wrong.)

Ahern offers a second analysis (pp. 27–28), but it depends on taking Hume's conception of a miracle to be that of a supernatural intervention into the natural order. Earlier, I argued that this incorrectly locates the point of application of Hume's emphasis on religion: it applies not to mark out a distinctive kind of cause but to make pertinent certain psychological propensities of human beings that will be appealed to in Hume's argument.

argument is viewed as a weighing argument that has nothing to do with the self-undermining considerations marshaled by Tillotson. But in fact, it is not difficult to recast Hume's argument as one that appeals to the notion of self-undermining. Assume we believe, on the basis of testimony, that a miraculous event occurred. We would then have to reject the lawlike claim with which this event conflicts. However, that presumed regularity had been placed beyond serious doubt by our experiences. Hence, we would need to rethink the evidential force of experience. But experience was our only basis for crediting testimony in the first place. Thus, in accepting the miraculous claim, we undercut our basis for accepting it.

This might appear to be thoroughly different from Hume's weighing argument, but in fact, they are closely related. Consider a situation in which someone is deliberating between two hypotheses, h_1 and h_2, whose support consists in varying amounts of data of a particular kind (e.g., observation). This person weighs the data, judges that more of it tells in favor of h_1, but concludes by believing h_2. On the weighing conception, this makes little sense: "We balance the opposite circumstances, which cause any doubt or uncertainty," Hume says, "and when we discover a superiority on any side, we incline to it."[13] Not to incline to h_1 is to affirm that the kind of data that favor it are not after all germane to deliberation. But such data are precisely one's basis for holding h_2. Thus, to incline to h_2 in the face of the balance of the data's tilting in the other direction effectively involves jettisoning what was one's evidential basis for h_2 in the first place. Once one appreciates that to spurn the results of a balancing of data is in effect to forswear the data's evidential relevance, one can appreciate why a failure, as Hume puts it, to "fix one's judgment"[14] in accordance with such a balancing leads to the "great absurdities"[15] of self-undermining that Tillotson describes.

In sum, we can recast Hume's argument in a Tillotsonian fashion. If we conclude that Jesus was resurrected, then in effect we shall be declaring the evidential irrelevance of experience, for we have far weightier experiential data that humans once dead remain dead than we do for the reliability of testimony to such extraordinary events. But

---

13. "Of Miracles," paragraph 6.
14. "Of Miracles," paragraph 4. Hume actually writes: ". . . he fixes his judgment. . . ."
15. Tillotson, *Works,* p. 314.

our only basis for crediting testimony at all is experiential. Hence, our inclining to the miracle deprives us of all reason to believe that it ever occurred. It is in this sense that, as Hume puts it, "the miracle destroys the credit of the testimony."[16] It is no wonder, then, that Hume at the outset cites Tillotson's argument as one of a "like nature" to his own.

3.2.   Hume had another model for such an argument, however, in a contemporary of Tillotson's whose works Hume no doubt read much more carefully: Locke. Toward the very end of his *Essay Concerning Human Understanding*, Locke considers whether Revelation—by which he understands the testimony of God[17]—could make it rational to believe anything "that is directly contrary to our clear and distinct Knowledge."[18] He says that it could not, despite the fact that Revelation "absolutely determines our Minds, and as perfectly excludes all wavering as our Knowledge it self." This seems like a paradox, for how can it be that "we may as well doubt of our own Being, as we can whether any Revelation from GOD be true,"[19] yet at the same time it be impossible that Revelation could ever bring us to believe something contrary to truths held obvious?

Locke's solution is that, while truths conveyed through Revelation command absolute assent, they can only do so once we have confirmed that they are being conveyed through Revelation—that is, through genuine testimony of God—and also "that we understand it right."[20] Hence, our confidence in the truths conveyed can really be "rationally no higher than the Evidence of its being a Revelation, and that this is the meaning of the Expressions it is delivered in."[21]

Locke in effect argues that a belief, formed on the basis of Revelation, that we are in error about some "clear and distinct" knowledge is a self-undermining belief. For holding such a belief must throw into doubt our judgment that what we have here is truly an instance of Revelation (since that judgment is formed on the basis of what we

---

16. "Of Miracles," paragraph 24.

17. John Locke, *An Essay Concerning Human Understanding*, Peter H. Nidditch (editor), Oxford, 1975, Book IV, Chapter XVI, Section 14, p. 667.

18. *An Essay Concerning Human Understanding*, Book IV, Chapter XVIII, Section 5, p. 692.

19. *An Essay Concerning Human Understanding*, Book IV, Chapter XVI, Section 14, p. 667.

20. *An Essay Concerning Human Understanding*, Book IV, Chapter XVI, Section 14, p. 667.

21. *An Essay Concerning Human Understanding*, Book IV, Chapter XVI, Section 14, p. 667.

deemed "clear and distinct" knowledge), and once that judgment is cast into doubt, we can no longer have any confidence in the original belief. To accept the self-undermining belief would, Locke says, "subvert the Principles, and Foundations of all Knowledge, Evidence, and Assent whatsoever"[22] and so of course subvert our very judgments that the testimony on which it is based is actually Revelation and that we have understood it properly. In other words, to accept the self-undermining belief would subvert our very basis for accepting it.

Thus, Locke's view is that no testimony from God could threaten the "Foundations of all Knowledge, Evidence, and Assent," for these form the only basis of our judgment that such-and-such is indeed an instance of Revelation—that is, an instance of a form of communication that must be believed. We can view Hume as generalizing this observation by arguing that no testimony from other people could threaten the evidential import of experience (through having us accept an event against whose occurrence experience speaks forcefully), for experience forms the only basis of our judgment that such testimony ought to be believed.

Locke was not in a position to extend his analysis in this way because he did not have an account of that to which human testimony owes its evidential value: as we saw earlier, Locke treated testimony as one of the "two foundations of Credibility." Locke might indeed have observed that no human testimony is likely to make it reasonable to believe anything "directly contrary" to the foundational force of testimony itself. But he has no basis for saying that such testimony will not favor belief in the occurrence of an event against which experience speaks overwhelmingly (a miracle for Hume), for he has no analysis of testimony's evidential force in terms of the evidential force of experience. Again, Locke has no account of the evidential force of testimony at all. Because Hume does offer precisely such an analysis, he can leverage these thoughts about self-undermining beliefs to arrive at conclusions about testimony's incapacity to make belief in miracles rational.

3.3.   Echoes of Tillotson's (and Locke's) self-undermining argument appear elsewhere in Hume's essay. In the course of his discussion in Part 2 about the strength of evidence for the reliability of testimony on

---

22. *An Essay Concerning Human Understanding*, Book IV, Chapter XVIII, Section 5, p. 692.

behalf of events deemed to be of religious significance, Hume makes four observations. I discussed the first three above (in Section 2.2), and we saw that they were psychological or broadly historical in nature. The fourth, however, has an entirely different character and is helpfully viewed as a kind of self-undermining argument: its point, as Hume puts it, is that testimony on behalf of miracles really "destroys itself."[23] Hume's argument is best quoted in full:

> To make this better understood, let us consider, that, in matters of religion, whatever is different is contrary; and that it is impossible the religions of ancient ROME, of TURKEY, of SIAM, and of CHINA should, all of them, be established on any solid foundation. Every miracle, therefore, pretended to have been wrought in any of these religions (and all of them abound in miracles), as its direct scope is to establish the particular system to which it is attributed; so has it the same force, though more indirectly, to overthrow every other system. In destroying a rival system, it likewise destroys the credit of those miracles, on which that system was established; so that all the prodigies of different religions are to be regarded as contrary facts, and the evidences of these prodigies, whether weak or strong, as opposite to each other. According to this method of reasoning, when we believe any miracle of MAHOMET or his successors, we have for our warrant the testimony of a few barbarous ARABIANS: And on the other hand, we are to regard the authority of TITUS LIVIUS, PLUTARCH, TACITUS, and, in short, of all the authors and witnesses, GRECIANS, CHINESE, and ROMAN CATHOLIC, who have related any miracle in their particular religion; I say, we are to regard their testimony in the same light as if they had mentioned that MAHOMETAN miracle, and had in express terms contradicted it, with the same certainty as they have for the miracle they relate.[24]

One way to understand this argument is via the following train of thought: *I believe in the epistemic significance of testimony on behalf of miracles, and on its basis, I have come to believe in the miracles of Roman Catholicism.*

23. "Of Miracles," paragraph 24.
24. "Of Miracles," paragraph 24.

Now, consider any miracle of Islam. It supports the doctrines of Islam, which in turn entail the falsity of Roman Catholic doctrines, including its miracles. Since evidence for the miracles of Islam consists of testimonial accounts, all such testimonies are in effect evidence against the Roman Catholic miracles. Indeed, testimonies on behalf of any miracle of any non-Roman Catholic religion are really evidence against the Roman Catholic miracles. These testimonies are epistemically on a par with the testimonies on behalf of Roman Catholic miracles, though far exceeding the latter in number. Consequently, since I do believe in the Roman Catholic miracles, it cannot be that I give any evidential credit to such testimony. But wait—such testimony is precisely my evidential basis for belief in the miracles of Roman Catholicism! Here, the judgment that testimony provides justification for belief in a miracle eventually undercuts one's confidence that it provides such justification. Or, as Hume puts it, "the testimony destroys itself."

I am not primarily concerned with the force of this particular argument. It certainly involves a number of assumptions that someone might disagree with—for instance, that the correctness of one religion is incompatible with that of another, that the incorrectness of a system of religion entails that its miracles never took place, etc. What interests me is instead that the argument can be understood to raise a complaint about a kind of self-undermining. Hume's point is that, given certain assumptions about the logical relationships among religious claims, the crediting of testimony on behalf of a foundational miracle leads to its discrediting.[25]

---

25. This fourth observation of Hume's is often passed over in silence, and where it is not, it is frequently given a hazy interpretation. For instance, C. D. Broad comments that the argument is "very ingenious," but its upshot, according to him, is that "the fact that miracles are alleged to occur in a number of incompatible religions tends to decrease the probability that miracles happen anywhere" ("Hume's Theory of the Credibility of Miracles," *Proceedings of the Aristotelian Society*, 1916–17, pp. 77–94; p. 81), a claim that hardly begins to elucidate Hume's conclusion that "the testimony [for miracles] destroys itself." Broad goes on to suggest that Hume's conclusion is that it cannot both be true that "[m]iracles occur in connection with [religion] R_1" and that "[m]iracles occur in connection with [religion] R_2." Thus, Hume's point, Broad says, is that "[t]he combined proposition implies its own contradictory and therefore *must* be false, and therefore *one* of the separate assertions *must* be false, and *both* may be" (p. 82). But who would deny this? Not the Christian who thinks the miracles of Islam never occurred.

A similar rendering is offered by Fogelin (*A Defense of Hume on Miracles*, p. 21), who writes that "Hume first notes that the miracles reported by different religions will stand in conflict with one another if they are intended, as they sometimes are, to establish the *unique* legitimacy of one religion over all others." Again, this does not speak to the purpose of Hume's noting this. Fogelin actually goes on to say that "[t]his is a nice point, but

The style of reasoning is similar to Hume's main point, as I have here interpreted it—namely, that belief in the occurrence of a (religious) miracle that is based on testimony is self-undermining. Hume writes "that not only the miracle destroys the credit of the testimony, but the testimony destroys itself"; though the remark may at first appear obscure, we can now see that he is in fact drawing a parallel between the two arguments.[26] Both arguments conclude that to believe a miracle has taken place must undermine one's confidence in the testimony that the miracle occurred. The main argument of "Of Miracles" depends on an analysis of the experiential underpinning of our confidence in testimony in general and on a few plausible psychological claims. It proceeds by showing that a belief in miraculous events must lead to a rejection of certain lawlike claims for which experience furnishes us with a proof and, consequently, to an undermining of our confidence in the evidential import of experience and so, ultimately, of the testimony that we thought justified our belief in the miracle. In this way, as we have seen, "the miracle destroys the credit of the testimony." The subsidiary argument in Part 2 instead makes use of assumptions about the logical and evidential relationships between religious claims. It proceeds by arguing that a belief in miraculous events must inevitably lead us to a rejection of all competing miracles and, eventually, to an undermining of the evidential import of precisely the kind of testimony that we thought supported our belief. Here, "testimony destroys itself."

Hume thought this self-undermining argument might strike his readers as "over subtle and refined," and perhaps this is why he preferred to present both his own main argument and Tillotson's in terms of the weighing of competing considerations. Nevertheless, he concludes that this self-undermining argument

---

I do not think it captures the full force of Hume's fourth consideration." But, as far as I can tell, Fogelin never does goes on to say what he takes its "full force" to be.

When Don Garrett comes to the conclusion of Hume's argument (*Cognition and Commitment in Hume's Philosophy*, Oxford, 1997, p. 150), he simply offers Hume's own words: "all the prodigies of different religions are to be regarded as contrary facts, and the evidence of those prodigies, whether weak or strong, as opposite to each other." But this does not explicate why the testimonial evidences' being "opposite to each other" leads to a peculiar difficulty in basing a belief in miracles on testimony; it fails to bring out Hume's thought that, given the logical relations between religions, establishing miracles on the basis of testimony inevitably backfires.

26. "Of Miracles," paragraph 24.

is not in reality different from the reasoning of a judge, who supposes, that the credit of two witnesses, maintaining a crime against any one, is destroyed by the testimony of two others, who affirm him to have been two hundred leagues distant, at the same instant when the crime is said to have been committed.[27]

Hume's example is a nice one in that it demonstrates how both the weighing and the self-undermining pictures can be employed. We might describe the judge as choosing to withhold judgment because the testimony of the first two witnesses is counterbalanced by the testimony of the second two. Or, we might take the judge to be reasoning as follows: *If I were to believe that the defendant committed the crime, I would in effect be judging that the testimony of the two eyewitnesses that put the defendant far from the crime is not sufficiently credible. But their report is evidentially on a par with the testimony that supports the claim that the defendant is guilty. Hence, I would in effect be renouncing the evidential pertinence of such reports. But wait—such reports constitute my only grounds for believing that the defendant is guilty!* The "over subtile and refined" argument, which we find here and in Tillotson, is, Hume points out, "not in reality different from" his own main argument or from the argument he attributes to Tillotson.

27. "Of Miracles," paragraph 24.

4

HUME AND TESTIMONY

4.1. In an essay on a raging controversy of his day that Hume himself suppressed, he had occasion to discuss an actual case of testimony on behalf of an extraordinary event. It will be instructive to examine this exercise, especially because it is easy to interpret the essay in ways that facilitate misunderstandings of Hume's position.

In the early 1760s, a Scottish poet, James Macpherson, published what he alleged to be translations of poems by a third-century Gaelic figure, Ossian, whose epic works had, according to Macpherson, been handed down orally and in fragments. The publications generated intense interest, both in Britain and abroad, and were prized by many, including Herder, Goethe, and Napoleon. But the poems also aroused immediate suspicion. By the end of the nineteenth century, it was widely accepted that Macpherson's translations were for the most part fraudulent.

While the Scottish Hume had "many particular reasons to believe these poems genuine, more than it is possible for any Englishman of letters to have," he confessed to a friend who was inquiring into their authenticity that he was "not entirely without my scruples on that head."[1] With time, these scruples developed into outright skepticism. In 1775, Hume finished work on an essay, "Of the Authenticity of Ossian's Poems," where he argued that it would be utterly irrational to believe in their authenticity.[2]

By 1763, Hume already believed that there were "internal reasons" favoring the fraudulence of the poems, having to do with their style, content, and the alleged manner of their preservation through the centuries. But his evaluation then was such that he thought the rationality of belief in the poems' authenticity might still be secured through the means of "particular" and "positive testimony from many different

---

1. Letter 215, to the Rev. Hugh Blair, September 19, 1763, in *The Letters of David Hume*, Volume I, J. Y. T. Greig (editor), Oxford, 1932, pp. 398–401; p. 399. Hume's earliest known letter on the poems, from 1760, is largely sympathetic to their authenticity (though already he registers a concern there); see Letter 176, to Sir David Dalrymple of Newhailes, Bart., August 16, 1760, in *The Letters of David Hume*, Volume I, pp. 328–31; p. 330. And a letter from 1761 still finds Hume introducing Macpherson to the publisher William Strahan as "a sensibile, modest young Fellow, a very good Scholar, and of unexceptionable Morals"; see Letter 183, to William Strahan, February 9, 1761, in *The Letters of David Hume*, Volume I, pp. 342–43.

2. E. C. Mossner dates the essay in his *The Life of David Hume* (second edition), Oxford, 2001, p. 419. The essay was never published by Hume but was found among his papers. Early biographers speculated that Hume withheld it out of consideration for the feelings of his friend, the Rev. Hugh Blair, who had singularly failed to follow Hume's advice on how to investigate carefully the poems' provenance and had published a much-reprinted analysis that deemed them to be authentic (in 1763, with an appendix in 1765 "containing a variety of undoubted testimonies establishing their authenticity"). It also bears noting that Samuel Johnson famously declared the poems fraudulent in his *A Journey to the Western Islands of Scotland* (1775). Perhaps Hume did not wish to publish anything that would associate him in the minds of uncritical readers with someone presumed to hold the Scots in low esteem.

Hume's essay "Of the Authenticity of Ossian's Poems" was printed in *Essays: Moral, Political, and Literary*, Volume II, T. H. Green & T. H. Grose (editors), Longmans, Green and Co., 1898, pp. 415–24. This essay does not appear in the Liberty Fund's edition of Hume's essays, which is puzzling because its editor states that the edition is "complete" and contains "the essays that were . . . suppressed by [Hume] during his lifetime" (pp. xvii, xix).

hands."[3] By the time Hume came to write his essay, however, his estimation had changed. First, it seems that his assessment of the force of the "internal reasons" that spoke against authenticity had hardened. In effect, he judged the poems' authenticity to be a "greater miracle" than he had beforehand: the evidence, in his view, now established "the utter incredibility of the fact."[4] This new judgment places even greater demands on testimony if it is to provide on balance a proof of the authenticity of the poems. "But will any man," Hume then asks,

> pretend to bring human testimony to prove, that above twenty thousand verses have been transmitted, by tradition and memory, during more than fifteen hundred years; . . . verses, too, which have not, in their subject, any thing alluring or inviting to the people, no miracle, no wonders, no superstitions, no useful instruction; a people, too, who, during twelve centuries, at least, of that period, had no writing, no alphabet; and who, even in the other three centuries, made very little use of that imperfect alphabet for any purpose; a people who, . . . [5]

Hume goes on to list many other considerations that in his estimation make authenticity highly unlikely.

One might interpret Hume as suggesting here that testimony is essentially incapable of providing a proof of a miraculous or even an extraordinary event. Such an interpretation would feed into the suspicion that Hume's argument about miracles is at root *a priori:* that it is in the very nature of a miracle to be unprovable by testimony. But this would be a mistake, for as we have seen already, in "Of Miracles" he writes that there is no contradiction in supposing testimony to be capable of bestowing such warrant. That said, under the best of circumstances, given the usual cognitive frailties of human beings, the proof that testimony is likely to afford an event is only so strong. Consequently, when the claim in question is one of "utter incredibility," like the authenticity of Ossian's poems, one cannot reasonably expect testimony to provide a net proof of it. Hume's point is that the evidence

---

3. Letter 215, to the Rev. Hugh Blair, pp. 399, 400.
4. "Of the Authenticity of Ossian's Poems," p. 416.
5. "Of the Authenticity of Ossian's Poems," p. 423 (ellipses are mine).

against the miracle of authenticity is so strong that testimony at its strongest will not furnish a net proof.

But in addition, we are far from the best of circumstances here. For the second respect in which Hume's estimation clearly altered was his evaluation of the strength of any testimony in favor of authenticity. Perhaps what struck him most was that the Highlanders testifying to authenticity were clearly delighted, if surprised, to be able to confirm that

> they were also possessed of an excellence which they never dreamt of, an elegant taste in poetry, and inherited from the most remote antiquity the finest compositions of that kind, far surpassing the popular traditional poems of any other language.[6]

Observation teaches us, Hume no doubt believed, that once the distorting effect of national pride is felt, testimony becomes evidentially worthless. "On such occasions," he writes, "the greatest cloud of witnesses makes no manner of evidence."[7]

Hume sums up the evidential impotence of testimony by Highlanders on behalf of the poems' authenticity in this way:

> But as finite added to finite never approaches a hair's breadth nearer to infinite, so a fact, incredible in itself, acquires not the smallest accession of probability by the accumulation of testimony.[8]

Again, there are materials here for potential confusion. In particular, that testimony cannot provide evidence for, let alone a proof of, an incredible event must not be thought of as a definitional truth. We know that Hume believes this is, in principle, possible. Hence, we must keep in mind the context of this summing up: a discussion of particular testimonies that he believes are so tainted by self-flattery and pride that they cannot be reckoned at all as being evidentially potent.

---

6. "Of the Authenticity of Ossian's Poems," p. 424.
7. "Of the Authenticity of Ossian's Poems," p. 424. Hume here uses the very same phrase, "cloud of witnesses," as he does in "Of Miracles," paragraph 27.
8. "Of the Authenticity of Ossian's Poems," p. 424.

In addition, Hume's finite/infinite metaphor is poorly chosen as a summary of the Ossian situation. First, the testimony in question here is precisely not of finite value. It is not as if testimony from a larger and larger collection of Highlanders should increase, even by a little, our reason for taking the Ossian poems to be authentic. However large, such a cloud of witnesses "makes no manner of evidence." Second, it is not helpful to say that the strength of our evidence in favor of fraudulence is infinite: this suggests that our judgment is unrevisable, undiminishable on the basis of further evidence, and this does not convey what Hume has in mind when he talks of a claim's being proven. If one must resort to an arithmetic metaphor here, perhaps Hume would have been better advised to have said that no amount of testimonials to the authenticity of Ossian, especially pride-infused ones, would make it rational for us to revise downward our conviction about the poems' fraudulence, just as zero added to zero never approaches a hair's breadth nearer to a finite quantity.

4.2.   I have stressed that one of the philosophical highlights in Part 1 of Hume's essay "Of Miracles" is its analysis of the rational basis of testimony-derived belief and of how such evidence ought to fit into the economy of belief revision. This account of testimony—that is, of the reason there is for believing on the basis of what others tell us— is one of the central, guiding conceptions of Hume's argument, and it has attracted a good deal of attention. As made clear above, Hume does not treat testimony as an epistemically *sui generis* method of arriving at justified belief. The epistemic clout carried by testimony is entirely derivative upon that possessed by induction, observation, and memory. Once the rationality of belief based on these three is granted, an argument can be fashioned to show why testimony-derived belief is justified. This is precisely what Hume seeks to do in the first part of the essay.

Hume's general point is that experience presents us with evidence for a presumptive law of nature that links testimony to truth. We can acquire information about what people are testifying to and about how the world is, and then we can see whether, on the whole and by and large, there is a correlation. If there is—and Hume thinks there is—then we have rational grounds to believe the testimony of others, and in just the same way that past observed correlations give us rational grounds for believing, on the basis of fresh mouse droppings, that a mouse is in the vicinity. Any rational confidence we have in the veracity of testimony ultimately rests on such empirical data. The rational basis of beliefs formed on the basis of testimony, Hume writes, "is derived from no other principle than our observation of the veracity of human testimony, and of the usual conformity of facts to the reports of witnesses."[9] In particular, no *a priori* reasoning can possibly give us a rational basis for thinking that testimony is to be trusted. "The reason," Hume says, "why we place any credit in witnesses and historians, is not derived from any *connexion* which we perceive *a priori,* between testimony and reality, but because we are accustomed to find a conformity between them."[10]

Sometimes Hume writes as if our belief in this "usual conformity" depends on our confidence in certain contingencies of human traits and capacities. For instance, were we not confident that humans are susceptible to shame upon being caught out in error or lies, we would not expect a connection between testimony and truth. But such confidence is likewise only obtainable through observation. Thus, Hume writes that testimony's

> connexion with any event seems, in itself, as little necessary as any other. Were not the memory tenacious to a certain degree; had not men commonly an inclination to truth and a principle of probity, were they not sensible to shame, when detected in a falsehood: Were not these, I say, discovered by *experience* to be qualities, inherent in human nature, we should never repose the least confidence in human testimony.[11]

---

9. "Of Miracles," in *An Enquiry Concerning Human Understanding* (critical edition), Tom L. Beauchamp (editor), Oxford, 2006, pp. 83–99; paragraph 5.

10. "Of Miracles," paragraph 8.

11. "Of Miracles," paragraph 8. This thought already appears in the *Treatise,* where Hume writes: "When we receive any matter of fact upon human testimony, our faith arises from the very same origin as our inferences from causes to effects, and from effects to causes; nor is there any thing but our *experience* of the governing principles of human nature, which can give us any assurance of the veracity of men" (*A Treatise of Human Nature* [second edition], L. A. Selby-Bigge, P. H. Nidditch [editors], Clarendon, 1978, Book I, Part III, Section IX, p. 113.)

Discovering these "qualities" likewise requires us to note certain patterns in the concatenation of events—for instance, that whenever someone has assured us of something that turned out to be incorrect, he has felt embarrassed. Thus, whether we make note of the conformity between testimony and truth directly or via observations of pertinent "qualities inherent in human nature," the crediting of testimony requires observation of how matters stand in the world.

It is at this juncture that an interesting objection to Hume has been raised.[12] For Hume writes as if it were a *completely* contingent matter that any pattern at all be observed. That is, the above passages suggest he allows that experience might reveal *no connection at all* between testimony and reality: we might discover, say, that there is no correlation between someone's telling us that such-and-such holds and its being the case that such-and-such holds. Hume seems to think that we might learn the meaning of someone's words and also discover that his or her claims are in error all of the time. But, this objection continues, it is in the nature of interpretation that this is impossible, for such an outcome must be held to count against the correctness of our interpretation. Quite simply, if my inquiry into what you mean reveals that what you tell me is mostly incorrect, then I need to revise my conclusions about what you are telling me. Too many mistakes no longer count as *mistakes*.

This point is a familiar one in recent philosophy (and much stressed by W. V. Quine and Donald Davidson), and it is often put in terms of interpreters' adoption of a principle of charity toward those whom they interpret. Describing the matter this way can make it appear as if this adoption is a courtesy, something interpreters do out of kindness or respect. But it is optional only in the sense that understanding another is; it is not optional if what one wants to be doing is *interpreting*. One may or may not choose to interpret, but if one does, then attribution of gross irrationality or error counts as some reason to rethink one's interpretation: the more obvious and systemic the failures, the stronger the reasons to revise. If this is the case, then any view that entails that it is possible for someone's testimony to be massively in error must be incorrect. And the objection to Hume is that his is precisely such a view. Insofar as Hume thinks that an interpreter's beliefs about what is true have no bearing at all on how to interpret what another is telling one,

---

12. A version of this objection is pursued at length by C. A. J. Coady in his *Testimony,* Oxford, 1992, Chapter 4.

Hume's conception of interpretation will fail to do justice to this constitutive element of interpretation.

4.3.   There is good reason, however, to conclude that Hume does *not* think this. Sprinkled throughout Hume's writings are intriguing remarks that suggest he well understood that some measure of reasonableness and correctness on the part of one's testifier is simply an artifact of the process of working out what he is testifying to. In fact, Hume may have been the first philosopher to have come to these insights, which proved to be so central to twentieth-century philosophy.

In his essay "Of the Dignity and Meanness of Human Nature," Hume considers someone who seems to affirm that he has no interest in friendship unless he can see how he might benefit. Hume writes:

> I am then confident that he abuses terms, and confounds
> the ideas of things; since it is impossible for any one to be so
> selfish, or rather so stupid, as to make no difference between
> one man and another, and give no preference to qualities,
> which engage his approbation and esteem.[13]

If someone appears to be "so stupid" as to say that he values something only insofar as it benefits him, then "he makes use of a different language from the rest of his countrymen, and calls not things by their proper names."[14] Some apparent stupidities are too great to count as real *stupidities*, and we must rather take them to indicate that, somewhere in the course of our working out what we had been told, we went off beam.

In fact, this constraint on attribution of belief, or interpretation of speech, was recognized by Hume early on. In *A Treatise of Human Nature*, he states the principle for the limiting case of outright contradiction:

> All we can say in excuse for this inconsistency is, that they
> really do not believe what they affirm concerning a future state;
> nor is there any better proof of it than the very inconsistency.[15]

---

13. "Of the Dignity and Meanness of Human Nature," reprinted in *Essays: Moral, Political, and Literary*, pp. 80–86; p. 84.
14. "Of the Dignity and Meanness of Human Nature," p. 85.
15. *A Treatise of Human Nature*, Book I, Part III, Section IX, p. 115. The inconsistency in question is that of the Roman Catholics who deplore religious violence against those whom they would condemn to eternal torment.

Clearly, Hume recognized that discovering what another is telling us is not like discerning tracks on the forest floor. At the outset of our inquiry, our judgments about these are not constrained by our beliefs regarding which animals are in the forest; the inquiry may proceed quite independently of those beliefs. But our judgments about what someone is telling us are always constrained by what we think is obviously reasonable and true. That our understanding of another results in imputing to him or her an obvious absurdity just establishes that our understanding is incorrect.

Hume also clearly does not think this principle is limited to inconsistencies, narrowly construed. We saw one instance of a more capacious conception of absurdity above. Hume offers another in an important passage from "Of the Standard of Taste," where he seeks to address an apparent problem for his view that the source of aesthetic and moral judgments is not reason but rather sentiment or the responses of observers. The alleged difficulty is that we find, at a certain level of generality, a great deal of agreement across people and cultures about such evaluations—far more agreement, in fact, than one would expect should these judgments ultimately rest upon our varying affective responses. Hume agrees that "[i]t is indeed obvious, that writers of all nations and all ages concur in applauding justice, humanity, magnanimity, prudence, veracity; and in blaming the opposite qualities."[16] But he suggests there may be an alternative explanation for this observed homogeneity, an explanation that does not trace the judgments to something, such as reason, that is shared by all people:

> But we must also allow that some part of the seeming harmony in morals may be accounted for from the very nature of language. The word *virtue,* with its equivalent in every tongue, implies praise; as that of *vice* does blame: And no one, without the most obvious and grossest impropriety, could affix reproach to a term, which in general acceptation is understood in a good sense; or bestow applause, where the idiom requires disapprobation.[17]

16. "Of the Standard of Taste," reprinted in *Essays: Moral, Political, and Literary,* pp. 226–49; p. 228.
17. "Of the Standard of Taste," p. 228.

We take implications to hold between certain judgments—say, that this action is a vicious one—and certain appraisals—say, that this action is blameworthy. These entailment relations are so obvious that, unless we understand another person's testimony in such a way that he or she too embraces them, we shall judge ourselves to have failed to understand that person. That everyone agrees courage is to be praised tells us more about how we interpret than it does about something common to all people from which such judgments flow.[18] Does it call for a substantive explanation, Hume asks, that we find Arabic writers agreeing with us about very general moral matters?

> But it is to be supposed, that the Arabic words, which correspond to the English equity, justice, temperance, meekness, charity, were such as, from the constant use of that tongue, must always be taken in a good sense; and it would have argued the greatest ignorance, not of morals, but of language, to have mentioned them with any epithets, besides those of applause and approbation.[19]

If someone is a competent speaker of Arabic and we interpret this person to be disapproving of justice, then we should conclude that we have misidentified the Arabic word that "corresponds to the English" word *justice*.

In sum, while Hume takes the project of understanding another to be an empirical one, it is in his view nevertheless constrained by the need to avoid imputing to the other beliefs that are obviously inconsistent, or that demonstrate confusion about obvious conceptual connections, or that display ignorance of such obvious facts about the world as to amount to spectacular stupidity. These side constraints guarantee, as a by-product of the process of interpretation, that another's

---

18. A similar point is made by Donald Davidson when he considers why people's choices approximate as well as they do to what rational choice theory would lead us to expect:
> The explanation for this is not that by luck or divine dispensation each of us has a share of reason; the explanation is rather that it is only in the environment of an at least roughly rational pattern that propositional attitudes can be said to exist. As interpreters, we cannot intelligibly describe or attribute propositional attitudes unless we know or believe they are arranged in an intelligible pattern. ("Expressing Evaluations," reprinted in his *Problems of Rationality,* Oxford, 2004, pp. 19–37; p. 28.)

19. "Of the Standard of Taste," p. 229.

testimony could not be completely in error. That much, Hume would himself insist, is an artifact of the process rather than an empirical discovery. Worries about Hume's view on that score should be dismissed.

But such results, Hume would also argue, will not take us far in determining the rationality of belief on the basis of testimony.[20] These

---

20. A notable instance of an attempt to extend what can be *a priori* justified is Tyler Burge's "Content Preservation," *The Philosophical Review*, vol. 102, no. 4, 1993, pp. 457–88. He argues that speakers are *a priori* justified in accepting as true what they are told "unless there are stronger reasons not to do so" (p. 469, italics omitted). The line of justification is complex and involves a raft of notions with which the ordinary speaker is in no way familiar. Nevertheless, Burge says, the justification *entitles* the speaker to believe. One may surmise that Hume, whose own justification does not rely on arguments beyond those already available to everyone, would have found this problematic. Of course, Hume's view does not require that the reasons people have be consciously appealed to as they form beliefs upon hearing testimony. He was not trying to describe the actual experience of coming to believe on the basis of testimony but rather the reasons for believing that a hearer has available to him or her. Burge's entitlements live at an even greater remove from the actual, for there is no sense in which such justifications need even be within the cognitive ken of the hearer.

Hume would also have been disposed to be skeptical of the *a priori* nature of the justification, for it presents us with the old problem of commensuration: if some evidence—say against believing in someone's testimony—is empirical in nature while some evidence is conceptual, how shall we weigh the one against the other? What sense can we attach to the comparison implicit in the phrase "stronger reasons"? For someone who thought it was a conceptual advance to have offered an analysis of the evidence in favor of testimony-derived beliefs that allows it to be weighed against the evidence that observation provides for candidates for natural laws, this question would have been salient.

For Hume, it was obvious that if empirical evidence could give one reason not to trust someone, then our evidence for trusting that person must be empirical as well. Burge rejects this: "Apriority has to do with the source of epistemic right; defeasibility is a further matter" (footnote 13 on p. 473). He insists that "the nature of the positive rational support for a belief"—say, that what this informant reports is true—is one thing, while the ways "in which a belief may be vulnerable to counterconsiderations" is an entirely independent matter (p. 461). If the source of the right does not justificationally rest upon any information provided by the senses, then it is *a priori*, according to Burge (e.g., see p. 458). It is natural to think, then, that an *a priori* epistemic right will obtain regardless of how the observable world happens to be, since how it happens to be is precisely what our senses tell us. But then it does seem pressing to explain how such a right could be empirically defeasible. That is, why might learning through observation how the world happens to be negatively bear on, let alone defeat, an epistemic right whose existence does not depend on how the world happens to be?

Perhaps Burge's picture is that, in such a situation, the *a priori* justification remains intact yet overruled by the empirical evidence. It is outweighed, not undermined. But in that case, we return to the point about commensurability. Hume agrees that our reasons to believe and not to believe are commensurable, but it is just because of this that he finds philosophical illumination in his analysis of the rational grounds for believing on the basis of testimony: it purports to make such commensuration intelligible. I am not here trying to resolve the matter so much as to sketch what the matter is.

side constraints can be met while allowing great variation in the reliability of another's testimony. And this reliability, according to Hume, can only be settled on the basis of empirical evidence.[21] Hume insists on the unintelligibility of attributions of total error, of gross irrationality, or of flagrant inconsistency and, at the same time, on the need for an *a posteriori* justification of testimony-derived beliefs.

4.4. The long history of reactions to Hume's remarks on testimony has seen other interesting objections. One set of concerns focuses on whether the account is an accurate description of how children learn to trust testimony. For instance, one might worry that it implausibly views the learning child as a proto-scientist who evaluates hypotheses as to whether a particular correlation is supported by the data. But of course this is not Hume's picture of how beliefs about general claims usually take root in us. When an event of one kind regularly follows another, we simply come to expect that this regularity will continue to hold: this "instinct or mechanical tendency"[22] is a product of our psychological makeup and not of any deliberate ratiocination on our parts.

An objection might still be raised that even this less theorized conception of the learning child's path to reliance on testimony is a fantasy. For while it might approximate how children come to believe that fire is hot—namely, repeated sightings of fire being accompanied by experiences of heat—the case of testimony's reliability appears different. This is because, while a learning child surely witnesses people saying how matters stand, one might wonder how often the child actually observes that matters indeed stand so. The worry is that very much of what a young child believes about the world is in fact acquired on the basis of

---

21. J. L. Austin was one of the first to question whether our general confidence in the testimony of others is to be justified on the basis of empirical evidence—perhaps even whether justification is the right kind of concept to bring to bear here at all. In "Other Minds," he considers the suggestion, Hume's really, "that we have in fact some basis for an induction about [some speaker's] reliability," that someone's testimony is best treated as "a sign or symptom" of how things stand. He calls these suggestions "dangerous and unhelpful," ones that seem "so obvious" at first blush but that, when taken too far, "become distortions." "[B]elieving in other persons, in authority and testimony," Austin suggests, "is an essential part of the act of communicating." (From "Other Minds," in *Philosophical Papers* [third edition], Oxford, 1979, pp. 76-116; pp. 114, 115.)

22. "Sceptical Solution of these Doubts," in *An Enquiry Concerning Human Understanding* (critical edition), Tom L. Beauchamp (editor), Oxford, 2006, pp. 35-45; paragraph 22.

testimony itself. Consequently, it is claimed, we must reject the simple picture according to which the child expects testimony to hold because that child has repeatedly observed instances of people's reporting that the world is so being correlated with the world's actually being so.

This worry about the adequacy of Hume's account taken as a description of how we, as young learners, actually come to rely on testimony can be extended to Hume's account taken as an analysis of why a given individual's testimony-derived beliefs are by and large justified. The question here is, regardless of how that individual actually arrived at those beliefs, whether on Hume's account that individual possesses materials that suffice for their justification. The question becomes sharper as we appreciate that Hume must think that the rationality of testimony-derived belief is to be grounded either in an individual's experience or in the experience of people at large. This is so because, first, Hume so grounds our reasoning concerning matters of fact and, second, he treats our inferences from testimony as "a particular instance" of such reasoning.[23] We have already remarked on the second point at length. Regarding the first, we need only recall that Hume holds that a person's inferences concerning matters of fact are typically supported by "events [which] are found, in all countries and all ages, to have been constantly conjoined together"—here, the evidence is clearly understood to be communal—as well as by events observed as part of "his past experience."[24]

In the context of a justification of testimony, these sources of justification can seem problematic. Communal evidence appears troublesome: an individual has no access to other people's observations save through their testimony, whose very reliability we are appealing to communal experience to vindicate. And personal experience appears insufficient: an individual does not ordinarily have the range of experiences needed to ground his or her confidence in testimony. The worry is that gathering the evidence needed to justify the reliability of testimony will inevitably beg questions about whether testimony is generally reliable.[25]

---

23. "Of Miracles," paragraph 5.

24. "Of Miracles," paragraphs 3 (italics added) and 4.

25. See George Campbell's *A Dissertation on Miracles* (originally published in 1762), reprinted in *Early Responses to Hume,* Volume 6 (second edition, revised), James Fieser (editor), Thoemmes, 2005, pp. 1–114, for perhaps the earliest such dissent. For a contemporary version, see Coady's *Testimony,* Chapter 4.

This raises large issues that I will not pursue here. It is worth noting, however, that the fact that an individual's inquiry into the reliability of testimony might at some point appeal to testimony-derived information does not by itself condemn the inquiry to circularity. Such a conclusion would be overhasty. For it may be that, at the point of appeal, justification for the reliability of such testimony has already been given. That is, a bootstrapping justification of testimony that proceeds in stages— where at each stage the justification of the kind of testimony now in question can make use of claims justified on the basis of testimony considered at earlier stages—remains an epistemic possibility. To show that it is not an option would of course require a substantive argument, beyond the bare warning about circularity. At this point, however, I shall bracket concerns about Hume's conception of testimony and turn instead to objections to the argument he fashions in terms of it.

5

OBJECTIONS TO HUME

5.1. With this analysis before us, it will be instructive to consider some interesting and occasionally long-standing objections to Hume. This will help bring his argument into focus and also situate it with respect to some of his other views.

While some critics are prepared to grant Hume's First Lemma, many have difficulties with the Second, repeated here:

> SECOND LEMMA: The falsehood of testimony on behalf of an alleged miraculous event of a religious nature is not "more miraculous" than the event itself.

Different kinds of dissent are possible here. One can accept this claim but insist that it has no interest at all since its truth is secured purely definitionally. Or, one can instead treat the claim as substantive—and false, either on the grounds that the evidential weight of testimony on behalf of a particular miraculous event is greater than Hume grants or because the evidential weight in favor of the regularity with which some miraculous event conflicts is less than Hume allows. I shall focus on each of these reservations in turn: exploring them leads to many of the historically prevalent objections to Hume's argument.

We understand the Second Lemma to mean that, "considered apart and in itself,"[1] the evidential weight of testimony on behalf of a miracle is not greater than the evidential weight in favor of the natural regularity with which the miracle conflicts. Now, it is tempting to think that this simply follows from the way Hume uses the term *miracle* and, thus, that this lemma can have no interest at all since in effect its truth is secured definitionally. For it is certainly true that the mere fact that some event is a miracle means there is a proof in favor of the natural regularity with which it conflicts. So much does indeed follow from Hume's conception of a miracle as an event that violates a lawlike claim for which evidence rises to the level of proof.

But for Hume, the existence of this proof does not settle the question of whether the testimony on behalf of the miracle outweighs the evidence in favor of the natural regularity with which it conflicts—that is, it does not settle how to judge whether the miracle occurred.[2] We have already noted Hume's insistence that there is no inconsistency in supposing testimonial evidence to provide a proof of an event that nevertheless conflicts with a lawlike claim for which we also have a proof. "There is no contradiction in saying," Hume wrote to a friend,

---

1. "Of Miracles," in *An Enquiry Concerning Human Understanding* (critical edition), Tom L. Beauchamp (editor), Oxford, 2006, pp. 83–99; paragraph 11. That is, bracketing temporarily the evidential relevance of the proof of the regularity with which the testified-to miracle conflicts. (See also footnote 22 in Chapter 2.)

2. Errors occur here even on the part of those sympathetic to Hume. For instance, Wootton writes that "[a]t the heart of the argument of 'Of miracles' is the claim that there exists a uniform course of nature which entitles us to dismiss miracles as improbable or even impossible events" ("Hume's 'Of Miracles': Probability and Irreligion," in *Studies in the Philosophy of the Scottish Enlightenment*, M. A. Stewart [editor], Oxford, 1990, pp. 191–229; p. 206). A miracle, as Hume uses the term, is an event that conflicts with some lawlike claim that is supported by uniform observations of nature. Hence, it is virtually definitional (barely a "claim") that a miracle is highly improbable: a miracle simply *is* an event that conflicts with a claim that is highly probable. Hume does not "dismiss" miracles simply on account of this improbability; there is much more to the argument than that.

that all the testimony which ever was really given for any miracle, or ever will be given, is a subject of derision; and yet forming a fiction or supposition of a testimony for a particular miracle, which might not only merit attention, but amount to a full proof of it.[3]

What Hume needs to argue for—and does—is that, in cases where a miraculous event touches upon religious concerns, it is most reasonable to think that testimony on behalf of the event will not "merit attention" in the slightest.

Now, imagine for a moment that testimony somehow succeeds in supplying a proof of a miracle—indeed, a more powerful proof than we have of the candidate natural law with which that miracle conflicts. As a wise man, I shall incline my belief toward that miracle and judge that it indeed took place. In doing so, however, an impediment arises to my continuing to treat that event as a miracle: I would in effect be judging that the balance of evidence supports rejection of the presumptive law with which the event in question conflicts. So, the event would not after all be in conflict with a claim for which my total evidence rises to the level of proof. But since that is what a miracle is, as Hume uses the term, I cannot henceforth think that the event in question is a miracle. For instance, if one comes to judge that, on balance, the evidence supports that Jesus was resurrected, then one must judge that, on balance, it tells against *Dead men remain dead,* the general claim with which it conflicts. But then one can no longer view Jesus' resurrection as a miracle, since there is no longer a proven general claim with which it conflicts. In short, if one judges that an event heretofore taken to be a miracle has occurred, one must immediately retract the appellation.[4]

---

3. Letter 188, to the Rev. Hugh Blair, 1761, in *The Letters of David Hume,* Volume I, in *The Letters of David Hume,* Volume 1, J. Y. T. Greig (editor), Oxford, 1932, pp. 349–51; pp. 349–50.
4. If explanations require reference to such proven lawlike claims, then presumably, should we decide on balance that a miracle has occurred, we would be without an explanation for it. (This presumes that our science is integrated in such a way that no well-confirmed lawlike claim covers an event that would falsify a well-confirmed lawlike claim.) Nothing follows about whether it is possible to explain the event, about whether eventually we might explain it. Therefore, Hume misspeaks when he writes to Blair that if we should have proof of a miracle, then "reasonable men would only conclude from this fact, that the machine of the globe was disordered during this time" (*The Letters of*

In a sense, therefore, it *is* trivially true that it is not rational to believe that a miracle has occurred: one cannot judge that an event has occurred which (one judges) conflicts with a presumptive law that one now has no reason to think is disconfirmed. Earlier, we saw that an immediate consequence of defining a miracle to be a violation of a natural law is that there are in fact no miracles. And now, we see that an immediate consequence of defining a miracle to be an event that violates a very strongly confirmed presumptive law is that we cannot consistently judge that an event has occurred and is actually a miracle. Undoubtedly, a recognition of this has fuelled the inextirpable suspicion that Hume has stacked the definitional deck in his favor.[5]

But the term *miracle* is actually getting in the way here, and this trivial truth—that once we have judged an event to have occurred we can no longer view it as a miracle—does not at all capture how Hume understands the thrust of his argument. Rather, his intended conclusion is that if an event of religious import would run counter to an overwhelmingly supported presumptive law, then no testimony will make it rational for us to conclude that event occurred. This is a substantive claim. Again, Hume's Theorem is not knowable *a priori*.

5.2.   Others have claimed not that the Second Lemma is trivially true, but instead that it is substantively false. Recall that Hume sought to balance the evidential weight of the testimony on behalf of a miracle "considered apart and in itself" against the weight of evidence in favor of the regularity with which the miraculous event conflicts. One can argue that Hume's weighing is flawed in either of two ways: first, that he has not given testimony on behalf of a miracle its due or, second, that he

---

David Hume, Volume I, p. 350). Rather, reasonable men ought only to conclude that they do not yet understand how the machine is ordered. This is in fact just the way Hume puts it in "Of Miracles," where he says of the imagined, well-testified-to total darkness that "our present philosophers . . . ought to search for the causes whence it might be derived" (paragraph 36).

In this connection, it is interesting to compare Wittgenstein's discussion of the relative and absolute senses of "miracle" in his "A Lecture on Ethics," reprinted in *Philosophical Occasions 1912–1951*, James C. Klagge and Alfred Nordmann (editors), Hackett, 1993, pp. 37–44.

5. For kindred misinterpretations, see, for example, Michael P. Levine's *Hume and the Problem of Miracles: A Solution*, Kluwer, 1989 (for instance, p. 149).

has given evidence in favor of the presumptive natural law with which the miracle conflicts more than its due. I will consider each in turn.

A quick glance at Hume's argument might leave one suspicious of his evaluation regarding the strength of testimony on behalf of miracles. For to show that the evidential import of testimony on behalf of a miracle is not as strong as some have thought, it might seem that Hume needs to establish that many occurrences of such testimony were not in fact correlated to the miracles reported. If so, then in arguing for the anemic evidential value of testimony on behalf of a miracle, Hume must assume that which he ultimately seeks to establish—namely, that miracles have not occurred.[6] We can put the objection this way: if the only way to cast doubt on the strength of testimony on behalf of miracles is to show there is little reason to believe that there have been miracles, then Hume cannot make the weakness of such testimony a part of the rational basis for rejecting the existence of miracles; that rejection would already be presupposed in arguing to the weakness of the testimony.

Note that, in the first place, this is a dialectically challenged response for most defenders of miracles. For even the most stalwart defender of miracles will acknowledge that many, if not most, miracle claims are indeed incorrect. So, it appears that this assumption, if indeed it were the basis for Hume's assessment of the reliability of miracle reports, is in fact shared by both Hume and those to whom he offers his argument.

But more importantly, the objection misconstrues the reasons Hume found persuasive. His argument is not that the relevant testimony is unreliable because it testifies to events that we know did not occur but rather that our information about the psychological propensities of human beings suggests we ought to put little stock in such testimony. As we have seen, what Hume argues in Part 2 of his essay is that what we know about human psychology should make us downgrade our confidence in the reliability of testimony on behalf of marvelous events, especially ones that are deemed by the testifier to have some religious significance.[7]

---

6. Paley suspected that Hume had cooked the books against miracles in this way. To "state concerning the fact in question," Paley says, "that no such thing was *ever* experienced, or that *universal* experience is against it, is to assume the subject of the controversy" (*A View of the Evidences of Christianity*, James Miller, 1860, p. 14). For several other instances of this objection, see Fogelin, *A Defence of Hume on Miracles*, Princeton, 2003, p. 19.

7. Once one appreciates the actual basis for Hume's assessment of the evidential weight of testimony on behalf of miracles "considered apart and in itself," one searches in vain in

5.3. A second family of objections to the correctness of the Second Lemma consists in arguments that the regularity with which a miraculous event conflicts is less well supported than Hume suggests. Such objections can take a number of different forms. To approach them, first consider a thought with which Hume could agree. While my present observation of the pineapple on the table directly supports a judgment that is in immediate conflict with the belief that there is now no pineapple in the vicinity, my present observation that this pineapple is not sweet does not support a judgment that is in immediate conflict with a belief about the sweetness of yesterday's pineapple. The conflict is mediated by a general claim supported by this belief—namely, that all pineapples are sweet. Hume insists that "past *Experience*, . . . can be allowed to give *direct* and *certain* information of those precise objects only, and that precise period of time, which fell under its cognizance."[8] Likewise,

---

Paley for countervailing considerations. Paley's own suggestions about the psychology of testifiers seem quite unpersuasive (see Paley's *A View of the Evidences of Christianity*, pp. 16–17).

Boswell quotes Samuel Johnson appealing to similar psychological considerations against Hume: "The miracles which prove it [the Christian religion] are attested by men who had no interest in deceiving us; but who, on the contrary were told that they should suffer persecution, and did actually lay down their lives in confirmation of the truth of the facts which they asserted. . . . This is a circumstance of great weight" (*The Life of Johnson*, 21 July 1763). In the same words, Johnson urges that "testimony has great weight, and casts the balance" in favor of Christianity (*The Life of Johnson*, 24 May 1763).

In general, Johnson weighted testimony highly. Once, he asked Boswell whether he had evidence that Canada was in possession of the British and imagined a skeptic about the matter. "Sir," Johnson said, "notwithstanding all these plausible objections, we have no doubt that Canada is really ours. Such is the weight of common testimony." And he added, "How much stronger are the evidences of the Christian religion!" (*The Life of Johnson*, 14 July 1763).

Ironically, Johnson might well have assented to Hume's First Lemma. Indeed, Johnson deploys *against Hume* an argument strikingly similar to Hume's own. Upon Boswell's suggestion that "the thought of annihilation gave Hume no pain," Johnson countered: "It was not so, Sir. He had a vanity in being thought easy. It is more probable that he should assume an appearance of ease, than so very improbable a thing should be, as a man not afraid of going (as, in spite of his delusive theory, he cannot be sure but he may go), into an unknown state, and not being uneasy at leaving all he knew" (*The Life of Johnson*, 16 September 1777). And Johnson adds mischievously, "you are to consider, that upon his own principle of annihilation he had no motive to speak the truth." (The irony of the situation is usually missed. For an exception, see Donald T. Siebert, Jr., "Johnson and Hume on Miracles," *Journal of the History of Ideas*, vol. 36, no. 3, 1975, pp. 543–47; p. 546.)

8. "Sceptical Doubts Concerning the Operations of the Understanding," in *An Enquiry Concerning Human Understanding* (critical edition), Tom L. Beauchamp (editor), Oxford, 2006, pp. 24–34; paragraph 16.

a miracle claim such as that of Jesus' resurrection is not in conflict with a judgment directly supported by any of Hume's experiences: after all, Hume never observed Jesus. The conflict is rather between the miracle claim and a particular candidate law (that people, once dead, remain so) for which Hume believes his experiences furnish a proof. There is no reason to think that Hume would have disagreed with any of this.

But at this juncture, three different objections suggest themselves. The first charges that Hume is mistaken about which general claims his experiences actually support. The second maintains that Hume here begs the question in taking the support his experiences provide for a candidate law to rise to the level of proof. And the third holds that Hume here falls into self-contradiction in taking his experiences to offer any support for any candidate law. I shall consider each in turn.

The first objection[9] can best be approached by reminding ourselves of what Hume had to say about the Indian prince who has never seen ice yet is told by reliable informants—say, travelers returning from Moscow—that they have seen solid water. While it may be rational, Hume says, for the Indian not to believe, on the basis of this testimony, that water can solidify, he should not judge the event to be a miracle. For while the event is indeed surprising, it does not contradict the general claim that the Indian's experiences support. Hume writes:

> Such an event, therefore, may be denominated *extraordinary*, and requires a pretty strong testimony, to render it credible to people in a warm climate: But still it is not *miraculous*, nor contrary to uniform experience of the course of nature in cases where all the circumstances are the same. The inhabitants of SUMATRA have always seen water fluid in their own climate, and the freezing of their rivers ought to be deemed a prodigy: But they never saw water in MUSCOVY during the winter; and therefore they cannot reasonably be positive what would there be the consequence.[10]

Hume's thought is that the Indian's past experiences do not prove the general claim *Water never becomes solid,* a claim that is indeed contradicted

---

9. The objection dates to at least 1762, for it appears in George Campbell's *A Dissertation on Miracles* (reprinted in *Early Responses to Hume,* Volume 6 [second edition, revised], James Fieser [editor], Thoemmes, 2005, pp. 1–114; p. 23).

10. "Of Miracles," footnote 22 (this is the second footnote of "Of Miracles").

by testimony to the existence of ice. Rather, they support such claims as *Water never becomes solid in India,* or perhaps *Water never becomes solid when above* t *degrees Fahrenheit,* etc.

Some critics of Hume have urged that a similar lesson be drawn in the case of traditional religious miracles, such as Jesus' resurrection. They have urged that Hume is wrong to think that these are miracles in his sense—that is, that they do not, in fact, violate law-like claims that our experience places beyond doubt. Rather, our experience furnishes us a proof of such claims as *Dead men who were not born of a virgin remain dead,* etc. Once Hume properly appreciates which general claim experience actually places beyond doubt, he will see that the event of Jesus' resurrection does not conflict with it and, consequently, that the evidence against the event is far weaker than Hume imagined.[11]

Hume did not consider this argument. Perhaps he thought it so obviously cut its nose off to spite its face. For the argument insulates Jesus' resurrection from counterevidence precisely by depriving it of the status of miracle. For what does its status as a miraculous event consist in, Hume might well ask, if not the fact that it confronts an overwhelming amount of evidence in favor of its nonoccurrence?

A deeper, less dialectical response to the objection would have led Hume to consider the kinds of questions that animated work on confirmation theory in the twentieth century, most notably those

---

11. For instance, J. Houston argues that the evidence Hume believes constitutes a proof of the relevant lawlike claim only does so if he assumes (illegitimately, in this context) that it is not rather evidence for a god who allows much regularity but occasionally causes disruptions to otherwise observed patterns in nature:

> So Hume reaches his conclusion that evidence for a supposed miracle will always be overridden because it will never outweigh the large body of (as Hume sees it) undeniably relevant evidence in favour of natural law, only by *assuming* that no god has acted miraculously in such a way as to produce an event of a kind contrary to natural law. (*Reported Miracles*, Cambridge, 1994, p. 134.)

Hume's taking the many cases of dead men remaining dead to be pertinent to whether Jesus remained dead requires, Houston says, "our excluding, at the outset of the evidence-weighing, the possibility that a god may on occasion order or bring about, and particularly on this occasion may have ordered or brought about, events which run counter to our general experience of nature" (p. 134). In effect, Houston suggests there is a "competing hypothesis" (p. 141) which is consistent with all the evidence Hume points to and which would not have us say that this evidence counts against the correctness of the testimony on behalf of an event that conflicts with our "natural law."

pursued by Nelson Goodman.[12] Our observations of many men who have died and stayed dead are observations of positive instances of the hypotheses that *Dead men remain dead* and that *Dead men not born of a virgin remain dead*. Now, which hypothesis should we adopt as a basis for judgments about undetermined cases—for instance, that of Jesus? Which hypothesis, as Goodman puts it, is projectible? Hume of course did not confront these questions head on. Though it is a credit to his discussion that it naturally leads us to take up these considerations, Hume himself did not help to resolve them. That said, they are of course not challenges specific to Hume's proposal: after all, everyone feels justified in judging that the next observed emerald will be green and not blue.[13]

5.4.   The second line of resistance grants that Hume's experience bears evidentially on the hypothesis Hume thinks it does but questions how strong this evidence really is. Why believe, this objection asks, that Hume's experience furnishes a proof of the relevant lawlike claim? Surely, most of Hume's evidence for candidates for laws—say, information about their instances—derives from the testimony of others. For instance, we can assume that Hume has not witnessed very many dead men remain dead. It is surely the testimony of others that provides him with most of the evidence he has for the general claim that *Dead men remain dead*. But if Hume insists on downgrading the value of testimony on behalf of miracles, he must do so across the board. If testimony does not count for much, then we must conclude after all that we lack anything like proofs of presumptive laws of nature. To repeat, if Hume has as little confidence in the value of testimony as his assessment of testimony on behalf of a miracle suggests, then he should not judge so highly the evidence in favor of the presumptive law with which that miracle conflicts, since that evidence likewise consists mostly of testimony. Putting the same point another way, if Hume values testimony on

---

12. See Goodman's *Fact, Fiction, and Forecast* (fourth edition), Harvard, 1983, p. 22.

13. Houston recognizes that his objection to Hume (see footnote 11) courts extrapolatory paralysis: for the "competing hypothes[es]" he says that Hume does not take seriously threaten to block our ordinary inductive inferences. His response is that "the god-intended import of these few extraordinary transgressions will readily be recognizable; and the recognition of that import removes any reason to question the presuppositions of the practice of enquiry" (*Reported Miracles,* p. 140). It is unclear to me how this response could satisfy Hume.

behalf of presumptive laws of nature, then he should equally credit testimony on behalf of miracles like the Resurrection and so should retract his assessment about the relative weakness of testimony on behalf of such miracles.

The objection can be framed as a dilemma for Hume: either he treats testimony on behalf of miracles on a par with testimony on behalf of presumptive laws of nature, or he does not. If he does, then he must acknowledge either that there is stronger evidence for miracles than he has allowed or that the evidence for the regularities with which the miracle conflicts is weaker than he has allowed. If he does not, then he begs the question by treating the testimonies differently. This pedigreed objection has proven to be most resilient, and versions of it appear regularly.[14]

Hume would grasp the second horn and insist he is not begging the question by valuing differently testimony on behalf of a religious miracle and testimony on behalf of the presumptive law of nature with which the miracle in question conflicts. Hume's judgment about the relative epistemic value of testimonies is not premised on the conclusion of his argument, Hume's Theorem (that it is not rational to believe, on the basis of testimony, that a religious miracle occurred). Nor is it based

---

14. Hume certainly knew of the objection. For instance, it was leveled (quite likely for the first time) by George Campbell in 1762 in his *A Dissertation on Miracles* (a draft of which Hume read), who charged

> that the experience may be *firm, uniform, unalterable,* there must be no contrary testimony whatever. Yet, by the author's own hypothesis, the miracles he would thus confute are supported by testimony. At the same time, to give strength to his argument, he is under a necessity of supposing, that there is no exception from the testimonies against them. Thus he falls into that paralogism, which is called *begging the question.* What he gives with one hand, he takes with the other. He admits, in opening his design, what in his argument he implicitly denies. . . . I leave it therefore to the author [Hume] to explain, with what consistency he can assert that the laws of nature are established by an uniform experience, (which experience is chiefly the result of testimony) and at the same time allow, that almost all human histories are full of the relations of miracles and prodigies, which are violations of those laws. (*A Dissertation on Miracles*, pp. 33–34.)

Fogelin (*A Defense of Hume on Miracles,* pp. 19–20, 37–88) judges that others have similarly objected, including C. S. Lewis and, more recently, David Johnson in his *Hume, Holism, and Miracles,* Cornell, 1999.

on the assumption that miracles have not occurred. The judgment about relative worth, as defended in Part 2 of Hume's essay, is based instead on observations about the psychological tendencies of human beings, such as the seductiveness of believing oneself to be the bearer of marvelous news, let alone news from a divine being. Reflecting on our experience with fellow humans and on our own propensities reveals a great difference between the reliability of testimony for the extraordinary and the reliability of testimony for the mundane. Thus, Hume can judge the evidential weight of testimonies differently without prejudging the issue in question: it is possible not to credit equally testimony for miracles and testimony for the ordinary without having to assume that the extraordinary never occurs or that it is never rational to believe, on the basis of testimony, that the extraordinary has occurred. In sum, this challenge to the Second Lemma does not succeed.

5.5.   I turn now to the third and final objection broached above, that Hume's views are inconsistent. This is an objection to *Hume's* deploying his argument against miracles, not to the argument itself.[15] One way of putting the objection is as follows: Hume cannot really fault a belief in miracles since his argument against its rationality is premised on the correctness of induction, which correctness Hume elsewhere rejects. Recall that for Hume's argument about miracles to work, he must assume that experience furnishes us with a proof (very powerful grounds) for believing in the presumptive laws of nature with which miracles conflict. That is, he must assume the legitimacy of inductive extrapolations from particular observations to general claims. But that induction is unjustified, the objection continues, is precisely what Hume himself infamously concludes in *An Enquiry Concerning Human Understanding*—ironically, the very locus of "Of Miracles" itself. Therefore, by his own lights, Hume's argument that a belief in miracles is irrational is defective.

The first point to note about this objection is that Hume would judge it incapable of saving the rationality of belief in miracles on the basis of testimony. One might put the point this way: either past experience does furnish us with a proof of certain lawlike claims, or it does not. If it does,

---

15. This objection is raised, for instance, by C. D. Broad; see his "Hume's Theory of the Credibility of Miracles," *Proceedings of the Aristotelian Society,* 1916–17, pp. 77–94; pp. 91–94.

then Hume's argument against the rationality of belief in miracles stands. If it does not, then such a belief still cannot be rationally defended, for it is premised on the evidential force of testimony, which (Hume insists) largely vanishes if past correlations between testimony and reality tell us nothing about whether such a correlation holds in general.

Well, maybe so, but the objector might still wonder why Hume adopts a different attitude toward those who believe that inductive extrapolations from past experiences are legitimate and those who believe in religious miracles on the basis of testimony. Hume clearly regards the latter as irrational in a way that the former is not. But why? If Hume were consistent, one might think, he should judge both parties to be equally irrational.[16] Has he not, after all, demonstrated in both cases a defectiveness in proposed justifications?

But there is an important difference in the nature of Hume's critical remarks about these two inferences: on the one hand, to general conclusions via induction and, on the other, to belief in miracles via testimony. To work our way toward it, recall the central thought that Hume believes rationally underwrites our inductive extrapolations: the thought that nature is regular.[17] It is because we believe that nature is regular that our past observations of fire's coinciding with heat make it rational to believe

---

16. Broad, for instance, writes that "Hume is really inconsistent in preferring a belief in the laws of nature based on constant experience to a belief in miracles based on the love of the wonderful" ("Hume's Theory of the Credibility of Miracles," p. 92).

17. What precisely the status of the thought that nature is regular is in the context of inductive inferences has been the subject of debate (as has the thought's precise formulation). Some treat it as I do here: a premise in an argument whose other premise is a claim about particular instances of a regularity and whose conclusion is a claim about the holding of the regularity in general. Others, however, treat the thought as something other than a premise: as background information in the light of which it is rational to judge that the warrant possessed by the claim about particular instances transfers to the conclusion. And views may vary about what a believer's epistemic relation to that information must be if the inference is to be rational, with some holding that the believer must have reason to believe the information is correct, some that the believer must have no reason to reject it, etc. The question is really how to understand the status of what Hume calls the "connecting proposition or intermediate step" ("Sceptical Doubts Concerning the Operations of the Understanding," Section 4, paragraph 17) or the critical "supposition" ("Sceptical Doubts Concerning the Operations of the Understanding," Section 4, paragraphs 19 and 21). I cannot enter here into the debate about which of these proposals is substantively different from the simple argument outlined in the text, or about which of the substantively different proposals is best viewed as the argument that Hume takes himself to be evaluating.

that all fire is hot. Hume famously asked how we might justify this critical assumption about nature's regularity. It is not uncommon to find students, when pressed to offer a reason for their conviction that the future will by and large resemble the past, pointing to the fact that it always has. And this is in fact the argument Hume considers.[18] He points out that it involves circular reasoning to the conclusion that nature is regular: for when we conclude, from our past observations that whenever regularities have held in the past they have continued to hold in the future, that in general regularities observed to hold will continue to hold, we are deploying yet another inductive argument and hence tacitly relying on the assumption that nature is regular—which unfortunately is in this case precisely what we were trying to justify.

Hume does not say that this is a fallacious argument. And indeed, it is not: it can be formalized as a piece of reasoning that involves a tacit premise about nature's regularity and that exhibits all the validity one could hope for. Furthermore, a fixed judgment of our "common life," to employ a ubiquitous phrase from the *Enquiry,* is indeed that the central thought—that nature is regular—is correct.[19] Hence, this argument is not only valid but sound.

Again, Hume's point is *not* that this simple argument in defense of nature's regularity is mistaken. Rather, what he helps us to see is that nothing like this argument could be our reason for believing that nature is regular, at least if we demand of such a reason that it have rational traction with those who are not already committed to something very like nature's regularity. Since part of our common life of reasoning is that we justify general claims about the world by appeal to inductive extrapolations from particular observations, our attempts to provide a justification for believing the general claim that nature is regular will themselves be inductive arguments and so will help themselves to the very thought we wish to justify. Though these justifications are of course sound (if uninteresting) by our lights, they could not possibly be so judged by anyone who was not already a party to our common practice of reasoning. Hence, their rational force cannot possibly be what induced us to participate in this practice in the first place. To use

---

18. See "Sceptical Doubts Concerning the Operations of the Understanding," Section 4, paragraphs 19 and 21.
19. "Sceptical Doubts Concerning the Operations of the Understanding," paragraphs 16 and 20.

Hume's words, we were not "engaged by arguments to put trust in past experience"; this trust was not initially "formed by reason."[20] Again, his analysis does not show that a particular reason for believing in nature's regularity is a bad one; rather, it establishes that a certain kind of argument could not be *our* reason, at least if a requirement on reasons be that they would have rational weight for someone who was not already a partner in our reasoning practices.

By contrast, the justification for belief in miracles on the basis of testimony is, from Hume's perspective, a dubious argument. This is the thrust of Hume's challenge in "Of Miracles." The justification needs to credit testimony on behalf of the miracle, but the only basis for this credit is experience, which when properly weighed actually favors the evidence against the testimony. Thus, if one were to heed the testimony, one would be forced to dismiss the epistemic significance of the only kind of consideration that makes it rational to attend to the testimony. The justification thereby undercuts itself and is the opposite, if you will, of the self-validating argument in favor of induction that Hume considers.

Still, even if Hume evaluates differently the simple argument for natural regularity and the testimonial argument for miracles, should he not, given his assessment of the first, likewise conclude that our belief in nature's regularity is irrational? Not unless a sufficient condition for irrationality is the unavailability of reasons that could be appreciated as such by someone not party to our common life. While it is debatable what, if anything, Hume thought on this score, it seems open to him to have held that a belief of ours need not be rejected as irrational simply because we lack reasons for it that could be appreciated as such from without our cognitive commitments. This could be because broadly circular reasons of an appropriate kind might suffice for the rationality of that belief.[21] Or, this could be because the obtaining of a certain kind of externalist condition distinct from possession of a reason might suffice for the rationality of that belief.[22] Or, it could be because that belief might be such an intrinsic part of the entire

---

20. "Sceptical Doubts Concerning the Operations of the Understanding," paragraphs 19 and 20.

21. Goodman urged such an approach to induction in *Fact, Fiction, and Forecast.*

22. For a defense of such an interpretation of Hume and further references, see, for example Louis E. Loeb's "Psychology, Epistemology, and Skepticism in Hume's Argument about Induction," *Synthese,* vol. 152, 2006, pp. 321–38.

epistemological apparatus presupposed by judgments of rationality or irrationality that it is not itself intelligibly assessable for rationality.[23] The important point here is to question the assumption that a necessary condition for rational belief is the possession of reasons that must be taken as such by anyone who lacks that belief.

In sum, what Hume actually suggests is that our belief that nature is regular cannot be justified by any argument that would be deemed sound by someone without such a commitment, and this suggestion is quite different in its epistemic consequences from his contention that appeal to testimony provides a *bad argument* for embracing a belief about miracles that he at present lacks. To claim of an argument that not everyone need be "engaged by" it is not the same as to judge that an argument is fallacious. The charge of inconsistency simply elides these important differences.

5.6.   These reflections might inspire a different kind of reaction to Hume's argument. In fact, just such a reaction makes a fleeting appearance during an exchange about Hume between James Boswell and Samuel Johnson. Though Johnson took testimony seriously, he was also famous (and feared) for his impatience with the credulous. Gesturing toward this standing reluctance to believe in reported extraordinary happenings, Boswell goaded the pious Johnson: "Sir, you come near Hume's argument against miracles, 'That it is more probable witnesses should lie, or be mistaken, than that they should happen.'" Johnson's response was brief but startling: "Why, Sir, Hume, taking the proposition simply, is right. But the Christian revelation is not proved by the miracles alone, but as connected with prophecies, *and with the doctrines in confirmation of which the miracles were wrought.*"[24]

---

23. Early suggestions along these lines can be found in Wittgenstein's *On Certainty* (G. E. M. Anscombe and G. H. von Wright [editors], Harper Torchbooks, 1972) and in P. F. Strawson's *Introduction to Logical Theory* (Methuen, 1952). The idea that the enterprise of rational assessment only comes into view once certain judgments are in place is worth spelling out in much further detail, both for its own merits and also as a potentially satisfying account of Hume.
24. *The Life of Johnson,* 22 September 1777; emphasis added. In Johnson's *Dictionary,* the definition given of *miracle* in its theological sense is "[a]n effect above human or natural power, performed in attestation of some truth" (quoted from *Samuel Johnson's Dictionary: Selections from the 1755 Work that Defined the English Language,* Jack Lynch [editor], Levenger, 2004, p. 331).

Johnson's comment will appear weak if we interpret him to be replying to Hume that evidence for the Christian doctrine extends beyond the occurrence of miracles. Johnson's appeal to prophecies, taken flatly, simply invites the response Hume offers in "Of Miracles"— namely, that only insofar as a foretelling of the future is miraculous is it an argument in favor of a religious doctrine, so an appeal to prophecies simply reduces to the appeal to miracles.[25]

But perhaps another way to understand Johnson is as claiming that the miracles of the Christian revelation are not proved by *the bare testimony on behalf of* these miracles. That is, we might take him as acknowledging that the inferential significance he accords the testimonies on behalf of the Christian miracles will not seem reasonable to someone who has not already embraced Christianity; the evidential significance of reports of miracles, Johnson may judge, will only come into view from the perspective of someone at home within the Christian faith, someone already working from within "the doctrines in confirmation of which the miracles were wrought." Christianity is a comprehensive doctrine that is not neutral with respect to what counts as a good argument. From outside this doctrine, reports of miracles will not be judged as persuasive evidence, but from within, they suffice for the Christian revelation to be "proved."

William James suggests that "the religious hypothesis gives to the world an expression which specifically determines our reactions, and makes them in a large part unlike what they might be on a purely naturalistic scheme of belief." If by "reactions" James allows our epistemic response to purported evidence, there is a clear kinship between his view and Johnson's. This is indeed suggested by his quip about John Henry Newman, who, he says, "goes over to Romanism, and finds all sorts of reasons good for staying there."[26]

In fact, variations on this thought have a long history. Joseph Hall, Bishop of Exeter and then Norwich, wrote in the early seventeenth

---

25. "Of Miracles," paragraph 41. Johnson's argument is so taken by, for instance, James E. Force in his "Hume and Johnson on Prophecy and Miracles: Historical Context," *Journal of the History of Ideas*, vol. 43, no. 3, 1982, pp. 463–75; p. 474. (Force's interpretation of Hume also falls short.)

26. William James, "The Will to Believe" reprinted in *Pragmatism and Other Writings*, Penguin, 2000, pp. 198–219; pp. 217, 204.

century that "[m]iracles must be judged by the doctrine, which they confirm; not the doctrine, by the miracles." Against the Roman Catholics, he argued that "they would prove the truth of their Church, by miracles; whereas they should prove their miracles, by the truth."[27] William Paley offers a pithy rendering: "once believe that there is a God, and miracles are not incredible."[28] Pascal too voices a similar thought, with impatience: "How I hate such foolishness as not believing in the Eucharist, etc. If the Gospel is true, if Jesus Christ is God, where is the difficulty?"[29]

Locke suggests that, if the right background of beliefs is in place, then the very improbability of the miracle should encourage assent to testimony on its behalf. He writes:

> Though the common experience and the ordinary course of things have justly a mighty influence on the minds of men, to make them give or refuse credit to anything proposed to their belief; yet there is one case wherein the strangeness of the fact lessens not the assent to a fair testimony of it. For where such supernatural events are suitable to ends aimed at by Him who has the power to change the course of nature, there, *under such circumstances,* that may be fitter to procure belief, by how much the more they are beyond or contrary to ordinary observation. This is the proper case of *miracles,* which, well attested, do not only find credit themselves, but give it also to other truths, which need such confirmation.[30]

It seems that Locke inhabits a framework of beliefs within which the very weight of evidence against the miracle can come to be viewed as rationally favoring the correctness of testimony on behalf of the miracle.

The idea even makes an appearance in the New Testament, which presents Jesus giving voice to a similar thought. When the Jews press him for direct evidence that he is the Christ, Jesus answers: "I told you,

27. Originally published in Hall's *Epistles* in 1608–11 and reprinted in his *Works,* Volume VIII, Josiah Pratt (editor), Whittingham, 1808, p. 135.

28. *A View of the Evidences of Christianity,* p. 15.

29. *Pensées* (revised edition), A. J. Krailsheimer (editor and translator), Penguin, 1995, p. 53.

30. John Locke, *An Essay Concerning Human Understanding,* Peter H. Nidditch (editor), Oxford, 1975, Book IV, Chapter XVI, Section 13, p. 667.

and ye believed not: the works that I do in my Father's name, they bear witness of me. But ye believe not, because ye are not of my sheep. . . . My sheep hear my voice."[31] To treat his works as evidence, Jesus tells us, requires that one already have gone some distance in the direction of what they are testifying to.

These last passages made an impression on Pascal, who quotes them repeatedly.[32] In general, he thought that there are good arguments on behalf of Christianity but that we are not in a position to recognize them "unless God inclines our hearts."[33] For instance, in the course of a remark on arguments that appeal to facts about the natural world, Pascal says that "those with living faith in their hearts can certainly see at once that everything which exists is entirely the work of the God they worship." However, when nature is examined by "those in whom this light has gone out and in whom we are trying to rekindle it," they find "only obscurity and darkness."[34] And perhaps the same applies to the arguments for belief based on the testimony of others, for Pascal several times quotes the plea from Psalms: "Incline my heart unto thy testimonies."[35]

In the following remarkable passage, Pascal appears to voice a view closely related to Hume's:

> M. de Roannez used to say: "The reasons occur to me afterwards, but first of all the thing pleases or shocks me without knowing why, and yet it shocks me for reasons I only discover later." But I do not think that it shocks for reasons we discover afterwards, but that we only discover the reasons because it does shock.[36]

The thought is highly compressed but seems to be this: de Roannez suggests that we are caused to react by reasons of which we are unaware. Only later are we able to understand the rational basis for our response. Thus, my heart inclines toward God for reasons that I do not at the moment consciously grasp; only afterward do I appreciate the reasons

---

31. John 10:25–27.
32. *Pensées*, pp. 259, 266.
33. *Pensées*, p. 110.
34. *Pensées*, p. 237.
35. Psalms 119:36; *Pensées*, pp. 111, 248.
36. *Pensées*, pp. 327–28.

that unconsciously led to my conversion. Pascal, however, wants to reject the idea that we can explain, at least in terms of reasons, my heart's inclination. What comes first is the inclination, and there is no use trying to ground it rationally in reasons that, unbeknownst to us, brought it about. If there is an explanation for our inclination at all, it will not be in terms of rational suasion unconsciously exercised. Once so inclined, however, reasons come into view for us—reasons that might serve, after the fact, to justify that inclination.

So understood, Pascal's conception is of a piece with Hume's view of induction. We find ourselves using induction, Hume thinks, on account of an "instinct or mechanical power" that so inclines us, not because we darkly respond to reasons in its favor.[37] Once in the thick of inductive practice, however, we judge it to be eminently rational. But any reasons we might then perceive in its favor were not—and could not have been— what inclined us to it in the first place.

But let us return to Johnson, whom I am interpreting as acknowl- edging that "Hume . . . is right" insofar as one should not hope to fashion an argument premised on reports of miracles that would ratio- nally persuade someone who did not already accept the Christian reve- lation to accept that revelation. Thus, Hume's essay, which seeks to provide the details of an "everlasting check" against such hopes, might have been acceptable to Johnson after all. Wittgenstein once observed that "*Very* intelligent and well-educated people believe in the story of creation in the Bible, while others hold it as proven false, and the grounds of the latter are well known to the former."[38] For instance, Johnson, a firm believer, once told Boswell "that all the things which David Hume has advanced against Christianity had passed through [Johnson's] own mind long before Hume wrote."[39] And not only had these arguments occurred to Johnson, he even thought that, in a certain sense, Hume "is right."

Yet ultimately, Hume's reasoning was of little threat to Johnson, precisely because it "[takes] the proposition simply." We can approach what may have been Johnson's posture by recalling again the situation

37. "Of the Reason of Animals," in *An Enquiry Concerning Human Understanding* (critical edition), Tom L. Beauchamp (editor), Oxford, 2006, pp. 79–82; Section 9, paragraph 6.
38. *On Certainty,* §336.
39. *Boswell's London Journal, 1762–1763,* p. 317.

Hume found himself in with respect to induction. Hume thought that observed correlations in nature only have evidential significance regarding unobserved cases for someone who already participates in our reasoning practices—in particular, someone for whom the rationality of inductive extrapolations goes without saying. Hume realized that this means we cannot fashion an argument premised on observed past natural regularities that would convince someone who does not already accept inductive extrapolations to accept them. Now, we might take Johnson to be similarly suggesting that a supporting consideration for Christian doctrine for someone who already accepted that doctrine might well not be a supporting consideration for someone who had not yet done so. Of course, it follows that such a consideration could not be someone's reason for accepting Christian revelation *ab initio*. But it would not follow that it could not be a reason for someone to accept the Christian doctrine unless one conceives of such reasons as capable of exerting a rational pull on anyone at all, wherever situated.

Perhaps Johnson's response to Hume can be put like this: once one recognizes that the proposition—about the rational bearing of testimonial evidence for miracles—need not be taken simply, one can appreciate that a belief in the Resurrection need be no worse off epistemically than a belief in induction. In neither case should one expect the availability of arguments that would have rational traction with those who are not already committed to the form of life, to lean on Wittgenstein's overworked phrase, within which those and kindred beliefs find a home. Instead, just as Hume, from within his common life, will judge that general claims about the natural world are "proved" (to use Hume's word) by specific experiences, so Johnson, from within his, will judge that the Christian revelation is "proved" (to use Johnson's word) by the reports of miracles and prophecies. One might say: distinctive forms of justification crystallize alongside the beliefs they justify.

Now, if Hume could be brought to agree that such a structural parity obtains, what kind of force ought it have regarding his rejection of a testimony-based belief in miracles? Must he conclude after all that his confidence in general empirical claims—that is, the conclusions of inductive inferences—is as well (or ill) grounded as Johnson's in the Christian doctrine? Some would have us conclude this. Perhaps James is calling for such epistemic ecumenism when he writes that we should cultivate "that spirit of inner tolerance without which all our outer tolerance is soulless, and which is empiricism's glory; then only shall we live and let live, in speculative as well as in practical things."[40]

Some, however, would urge that for Hume to take seriously such an "inner tolerance" would be for him to try to occupy a radically disengaged position from which he could evenhandedly judge that the common life within which he moves and that within which Johnson does are fully on a par. And they would insist that no sooner is the scenario made explicit than we can see it to be a will-o'-the-wisp. To be able to think and judge is to be immersed in a particular practice, to take seriously its commitments and forms of reasoning. The philosopher who most insistently reminds us of this is Quine:

> Have we now so far lowered our sights as to settle for a relativistic doctrine of truth—rating the statements of each theory as true for that theory, and brooking no higher criticism? Not so. The saving consideration is that we continue to take seriously our own particular aggregate science, our own particular world-theory or loose total fabric of quasi-theories, whatever it may be. Unlike Descartes, we own and use our beliefs of the moment, even in the midst of philosophizing, until by what is vaguely called scientific method we change them here and there for the better. Within our own total evolving doctrine, we can judge truth as earnestly and absolutely as can be; subject to correction, but that goes without saying.[41]

If Quine is right, there are limits to the epistemic toleration that James enjoins, and Hume cannot after all view these judgments as if from nowhere. From within the common life that defines his epistemic commitments and his standards of reason, Hume must deem Johnson's judgment about the rational support for miracles either incorrect or not fully intelligible. The parity of their respective positions is merely formal. For there is a substantive asymmetry induced by the critical fact that Hume comes to these issues already a member of one flock and not the other.

---

40. "The Will to Believe," p. 218.
41. W. V. Quine, *Word and Object*, MIT, 1960, pp. 24–25. For some reflections on this feature of Quine's thought, see Alexander George, "Quine's Indeterminacy: A Paradox Resolved and a Problem Revealed," *The Harvard Review of Philosophy*, vol. 21, 2014, pp. 41–55.

6

TOO BIG FOR A BLUNDER?

6.1.   In 1890, Sir James Frazer, a Scottish anthropologist at Cambridge University, began to publish what was to become his magnum opus, *The Golden Bough,* a comparative study of so-called primitive religions and rituals. The last of its twelve volumes appeared in 1915, with a final, supplementary volume in 1936. The work was enormously influential, not only among anthropologists but also with writers, artists, and the educated public, who were beguiled by the extraordinary practices and beliefs described by Frazer and impressed by the framework of human development he presented in his attempt to make these strange ways of acting and thinking intelligible to himself and his readers.

Wittgenstein was intrigued by the work, had a friend read selections to him, and eventually received his own abridged, one-volume copy. Over many years, Wittgenstein jotted down thoughts about Frazer, which were eventually collected and published after his death. They are not often read, and perhaps even less often appreciated. I shall begin by touching on several themes in these remarks, with a view to explaining, eventually, the illumination that they cast upon Hume's work on religion.

Frazer presents himself as offering an empirical hypothesis about the origins of certain magical practices. One of his leading ideas is that primitive people are best viewed as scientists seeking to understand the workings of their natural environment by developing testable theories that can be used to predict and control the natural events around them—except that, being primitive people, their theories of the workings of nature are themselves primitive. Much of magic and ritual, Frazer suggests (or at least Wittgenstein so understood him) are the results of proto-scientific inquiry into the workings of the natural world by people who have very little to go on.

Many find such historical hypotheses to be plausible, sometimes even compelling explanations for certain ritualistic activities. Consider, for instance, the fact that many Jews shun pork. This can seem very puzzling: why should there be such an avoidance of the eating of pigs? People will often respond that Jews proscribe pork because, a very long time ago, it was believed that pigs were unclean animals, carriers of diseases deadly to humans, and therefore dangerous to eat. The practice, it is insisted, was actually born from an empirical hypothesis on the part of the Ancient Jews about the kinds of food that are hazardous to one's health, a hypothesis which eventually fossilized into a ritualistic prohibition.

This is just the kind of stance that Frazer adopts toward the puzzlement many of us experience when confronted by ancient practices. I shall focus on three thematic responses to this stance in Wittgenstein's work.[1] The first is simply that Frazer's explanations for the genesis of these practices are unsatisfactory. Again, these explanations treat many religious beliefs and rituals as expressing—or being a consequence of—empirical hypotheses about the natural world; for instance, the tribe engages in a particular ritual dance because its members believe that doing so will bring rain. Wittgenstein insists, however, that attribution of such a belief, viewed as an empirical hypothesis on the part of the

---

1. My thinking about Wittgenstein's remarks on Frazer have been deepened by the work of Frank Cioffi; see his *Wittgenstein on Freud and Frazer,* Cambridge University Press, 1998.

members of the tribe, is misguided. This is because such an attribution simply makes the natives into exceedingly dim individuals—so dim, in fact, that the attribution loses its plausibility. In an extraordinary passage, Wittgenstein takes a common explanation for the longevity of superstition and turns it on its head to suggest that the entire form of explanation is spurious. He writes:

> Frazer says that it is very hard to discover the error in magic—and that is why it has lasted so long—because, for example, an incantation that is supposed to bring rain certainly seems efficacious sooner or later. But then it is surely remarkable that people don't realize earlier that sooner or later it's going to rain anyhow.[2]

Frazer imagines our ancestors to be forensically sophisticated enough to seek out confirmation for their hypotheses but, at the same time, so clueless as not to appreciate "that sooner or later it's going to rain anyhow." When Wittgenstein observes that "toward morning, when the sun is about to rise, rites of daybreak are celebrated by the people, but not during the night, when they simply burn lamps," it is to suggest that such rites could not possibly be performed with a view to hastening the dawn. Therefore, such rites are not meaningfully criticized as the product of incorrect views about the natural world. Likewise, baptism is not helpfully understood as arising from beliefs about the salutary effects of cleansing: "Baptism as washing.——An error arises only when magic is interpreted scientifically." À propos another ritual, Wittgenstein remarks:

> If the adoption of a child proceeds in such a way that the mother draws it from under her clothes, it is surely insane to believe that an error is present and that she believes she has given birth to the child.[3]

Again, to interpret the practice as stemming from an empirical belief is to completely misunderstand it. Indeed, it is not to form a fully intelligible understanding of it at all.

---

2. "Remarks on Frazer's *Golden Bough*," in Ludwig Wittgenstein, *Philosophical Occasions: 1912–1951,* James Klagge and Alfred Nordmann (editors), Hackett, 1993, pp. 119–59; p. 121.
3. "Remarks on Frazer's *Golden Bough,*" pp. 137, 125.

Wittgenstein's point here is in fact related to an insight that, I claimed earlier, we first encounter in Hume: that no man could be, as Hume puts it, "so stupid" as to "give no preference to qualities, which engage his approbation."[4] To think someone could fail to give such a preference is not to be ignorant of the limits of stupidity but rather, as Hume says, to betray "the greatest of ignorance . . . of language."[5] We simply do not use the terms *preference* and *approbation* in such a way that we affirm the possibility of one's having a preference for something of which one in no way approves. And likewise, no humans, however primitive, could be "so stupid" as not to realize that daybreak cannot be hastened, or that "sooner or later it's going to rain anyhow."

Yet another reason for suspecting the inadequacy of Frazer's construal of religious beliefs is that they are simply not surrounded by enough trappings of what we call "empirical hypotheses." This too is hinted at by Wittgenstein when he observes:

> It can indeed happen, and often does today, that a person
> will give up a practice after he has recognized an error on
> which it was based. . . . But this is not the case with the reli-
> gious practices of a people and *therefore* there is *no* question
> of an error.[6]

I take his point to be this: empirical conjectures typically are tested against observable data, evaluated against competitors, modified over time, pruned of extraneous assumptions, etc. The beliefs that Frazer focuses on are singularly not like this. One might be able to recast them in such a way that they bear a superficial resemblance to paradigmatic empirical hypotheses, but if one attends to the role the beliefs play in the lives of those who hold them, a world of difference can be appreciated, producing a hesitation to call them "empirical conjectures."

To illustrate these two points in action, consider the force they have in connection with common speculations about the genesis of the

---

4. "Of the Dignity and Meanness of Human Nature," reprinted in *Essays: Moral, Political, and Literary* (revised edition), Eugene F. Miller (editor), Liberty Fund, 1987, pp. 80-86; p. 84.
5. "Of the Standard of Taste," reprinted in *Essays: Moral, Political, and Literary*, pp. 226-49; p. 229.
6. "Remarks on Frazer's *Golden Bough*," p. 121. He adds: "Rather, the characteristic feature of ritualistic action is not at all a view, an opinion, whether true or false, although an opinion—a belief—can itself be ritualistic or part of a rite" (p. 129).

proscription on pork. Does it make sense to say of a people who were intelligent enough to engage in sophisticated animal husbandry, and who had the opportunity to observe a rich pattern of foodborne illness and its relation to animals and cooking techniques, that a reasonable conclusion on their part was that the eating of pigs ought to be unconditionally shunned for health reasons? If the Ancient Jews were astute enough to discover the link between trichinosis and the consumption of pigs—not a trivial feat given the varied and sometimes prolonged incubation period of the parasite—then one might expect them to have been astute enough to realize that trichinosis from pigs can be avoided by steering clear of raw or undercooked meat.

In addition, is it plausible to think that those early Jews treated this proscription as stemming from an empirical conjecture subject to revision, refinement, or rejection in the light of further testing? If it had been so treated, it would surely not have survived long. This proscription on consumption was interwoven with many others whose assimilation to empirical conjectures regarding dietary health is even more far-fetched, such as the proscription on the eating of fruit from trees less than four years old, on the mixing of meat and milk, and on and on. These regulations played a complex role in the lives of the early Jews, a role not happily assimilated to that of empirical hypotheses about the source of a disease. One suspects that if the Ancient Jews had been asked to justify their practice, their answer would not have involved theories about what promotes human health but would instead have been that God forbade the consumption of pigs, period.

6.2.   The second response to Frazer that one finds in Wittgenstein remains even if one were to reject this last criticism. This response contends that Frazer's inquiry deflects our attention from the questions that we truly want addressed concerning many beliefs and rituals. Wittgenstein faults Frazer not merely for offering an inadequate empirical account of the phenomena that can seem so puzzling but also for offering the wrong kind of response to our puzzlement. Why is it the wrong kind of response? Because it misunderstands the nature of the puzzlement.

Without a doubt, the world can present us with phenomena that demand the acquisition of further knowledge, the elaboration of explanatory frameworks, and the development of theories. In most places on Earth, for instance, the number of hours of sunlight shifts each day. This is puzzling, and undoubtedly, it puzzled our ancestors. The puzzlement was only relieved when we acquired a deeper knowledge, in the form of a theory of celestial motion, that explains the observed phenomena. Wittgenstein points out, however, "that there is puzzlement and mental discomfort, not only when our curiosity about certain facts is not satisfied or when we can't find a law of nature fitting in with all our experience."[7] For there is also the kind of puzzlement elicited by some of Frazer's descriptions of magical rites and beliefs. Here, someone might feel as if he had witnessed something sinister or uncomfortable or disturbing in some elusive way. Wittgenstein's second objection to Frazer is that even if his empirical hypotheses as to the genesis of these practices were correct, they would not be of use to someone who struggles to accommodate these facts about human life. The charge, then, is that Frazer misunderstands the nature of the bewilderment that confronts some of us upon considering the practices that he describes.

One might wonder whether Wittgenstein is fair to suggest not only that Frazer's responses are inadequate but also that the very questions Frazer seeks to answer—namely, the empirical origins of these practices—are the wrong ones to ask. For perhaps Frazer really was interested in empirical questions about development; perhaps Frazer did not feel disturbed by these practices and so saw no need to provide an account of a consolatory nature. Wittgenstein would not have agreed. He says: "When Frazer begins by telling us the story of the King of the Wood of Nemi, he does this in a tone which shows that he feels, and wants us to feel, that something strange and dreadful is happening."[8] And indeed, we can hear what Wittgenstein points to when Frazer imagines the "strange and recurring tragedy" priests had to endure to become King of the Wood:

> [S]et to melancholy music the background of forest showing
> black and jagged against a lowering and stormy sky, the
> sighing of the wind in the branches, the rustle of withered
> leaves under foot, the lapping of cold water upon the shore,

---

7. *The Blue Book,* Blackwell, Oxford, 1964, p. 59.
8. "Remarks on Frazer's *Golden Bough*," p. 121.

and in the foreground, pacing to and fro, now in twilight
and now in gloom, a dark figure with a glitter of steel at the
shoulder whenever the pale moon, riding clear of the cloud-
rack, peers down at him through the matted boughs.[9]

But whether Frazer cheated himself or not, his explanations do not
touch what Wittgenstein felt *he* wanted addressed. Frazer's empirical
conjectures, writes Wittgenstein, "will be of little help to someone, say,
who is upset because of love.——It will not calm him."[10] This remark
reminds us that we do not need to turn to such exotica as ancient sacri-
ficial rituals for examples of the kind of bewilderment for which empirical conjectures provide no relief. Life throws them our way with seeming
alacrity.

Rush Rhees, one of Wittgenstein's students and friends, suggests a
nice example. As he points out, "A man may wonder what to make of his
life. He may be bewildered by the sort of person he finds himself to be."[11]
This bewilderment is given a fine expression in the Talking Heads' song
"Once in a Lifetime," in which David Byrne sings:

And you may find yourself living in a shotgun shack.
And you may find yourself in another part of the world.
And you may find yourself behind the wheel of a large automobile.
And you may find yourself in a beautiful house, with a beautiful wife.
And you may ask yourself Well . . . How did I get here?

This voices well the experience of someone astonished that life should
have come to have the contours that it does. And when, perplexed and
disturbed, he asks "Well, . . . How did I get here?" he will not be com-
forted by being reminded of his choices, of how he came to buy that
large automobile, or how he met and wooed his beautiful wife. Whatever
it is that this person is after, it is likely not more facts.

Or let us consider another example closer to our subject. James
Boswell found himself very disturbed by Hume's reputation as the
Great Infidel. He was not disturbed that people thought this of Hume,
for Boswell thought this himself—and that was precisely what disturbed

9. *The New Golden Bough,* Theodor H. Gaster (editor), Criterion, 1959, pp. 3–4.
10. "Remarks on Frazer's *Golden Bough,*" p. 123.
11. Rush Rhees, "Sexuality," in *Moral Questions,* St. Martin's Press, 1999, pp. 139–50; p. 142.

him. He could not understand how such "a civil, sensible, and comfortable looking man" could fail to believe in a Providential state, could think that complete and permanent annihilation was his lot.[12] Indeed, as Hume lay dying, Boswell paid him a last visit in the hopes of learning something from him that would set Boswell's mind at ease. The visit did not have its intended effect, and Boswell records that he left Hume "with impressions which disturbed me for some time."[13] Whatever it was that "disturbed" Boswell about Hume's lack of religious belief, it could not be helpfully addressed through the acquisition of yet more information about Hume.

One last example before leaving this point. One of Wittgenstein's great recurring themes is that yet another source for this kind of bewilderment is philosophical reflection itself. In the very early hours of such reflection, we often find ourselves confronted by a puzzlement that troubles us, perhaps to the point of precipitating a lifetime of inquiry. But philosophers typically misunderstand the nature of their troubles, Wittgenstein suggests, and seek relief in the acquisition of further knowledge, usually through the construction of philosophical theories that draw upon the natural sciences both for inspiration and information:

> For what struck *us* as being queer about thought and thinking was not at all that it had curious effects which we were not yet able to explain (causally). Our problem, in other words, was not a scientific one; but a muddle felt as a problem. . . . And when we are worried about the nature of thinking, the puzzlement which we wrongly interpret to be one about the nature of a medium is a puzzlement caused by the mystifying use of our language.[14]

For Wittgenstein, philosophical troubles are not like the challenges raised by the natural world. St. Augustine's torments about time cannot be calmed through a theoretical inquiry into some subject matter, as could Newton's puzzlement about the tides. If philosophical agitation can be laid to rest at all, it will have to be in some other way.

---

12. Quoted in E. C. Mossner, *The Life of David Hume,* Oxford, 1980, p. 588.
13. Quoted in *The Life of David Hume,* p. 598 (see also Boswell's account of his dream about Hume after his death, p. 606).
14. *The Blue Book,* p. 6.

6.3.   This brings me to the third thought I would like to draw from Wittgenstein: his suggestion about how those whose bewilderment will not yield to theorizing might after all be consoled. He says in the context of a discussion of Frazer's rituals that a "perspicuous representation brings about the understanding which consists precisely in the fact that we 'see the connections.' "[15] In particular, he says, the connections with "our own feelings and thoughts."[16] I take Wittgenstein to be suggesting that we can achieve a certain solace when confronted by a disturbing practice through an understanding born from seeing clearly the practice's complex connections to our own reactions and thoughts. For instance, writing of the significance of the Beltane Fire Festivals, Wittgenstein says that

> what I see in those stories is nevertheless acquired through the evidence, including such evidence as does not appear to be directly connected with them,—through the thoughts of man and his past, through all the strange things I see, and have seen and heard about, in myself and others.[17]

We are usually only dimly aware of these connections, and it can be a struggle to see them clearly. This tangle of associations, he says, forms "[t]he crowd of thoughts which cannot come out, because they all want to rush forward and thus get stuck in the exit."[18] Wittgenstein's suggestion is that sometimes a disturbing befuddlement can be eased by helping such a tangled mass of connections out the door.

Others too have found value in such a pursuit. William Hazlitt said of great poetry what Wittgenstein believed about a certain kind of comfort, that it "can only be produced by unravelling the real web of associations, which have been wound round any subject by nature, and the unavoidable conditions of humanity."[19] In a strikingly similar passage, Keats wrote of "a gordian complication of feelings, which must take

---

15. "Remarks on Frazer's *Golden Bough*," p. 133. Compare from *Philosophical Investigations* (third edition), G. E. M. Anscombe (translator), Macmillan, 1968, §122: "A perspicuous representation produces just that understanding which consists in 'seeing connexions.' "
16. "Remarks on Frazer's *Golden Bough*," p. 143.
17. "Remarks on Frazer's *Golden Bough*," p. 151.
18. "Remarks on Frazer's *Golden Bough*," p. 123.
19. William Hazlitt, "Pope, Lord Byron, and Mr. Bowles," in *The Collected Works of William Hazlitt: Fugitive Writings: Fugitive Writings*, 11:486–507. London: J.M. Dent & Co., 1904.,

time to unravel and care to keep it unravelled."[20] And as usual, Samuel Johnson was already there when he suggested that "it is not sufficiently considered, that men more frequently require to be reminded than informed."[21]

Might this form of clarification, which consists of being reminded of what we already know instead of being informed of news, prove to be more helpful to those who find themselves uncomfortably perplexed by the ancient Jewish proscription against the eating of pork? I am speaking about those who find speculations about the proto-scientific hypothesizing of Jews long ago not only unpersuasive but also irrelevant to understanding the odd resonances this practice has for them. For such people, it might be more illuminating to reflect on, as Wittgenstein puts it, "a tendency in ourselves."[22] For instance, it is clear, he says, that there

> are dangers connected with eating and drinking, not only
> for savages but also for us; nothing is more natural than
> the desire to protect oneself from these; and now we could
> devise such preventative measures ourselves—But accord-
> ing to what principle are we to invent them? Obviously,
> according to the one by which all dangers are reduced to the
> form of a few very simple ones which are immediately evi-
> dent to man. . . . Personification will, of course, play a large
> role in these simple pictures, for, as everyone knows, men
> (hence spirits) can become dangerous to mankind.[23]

If we take this "tendency in ourselves" and place it alongside our responses to pigs, our natural comparisons between them and men, then perhaps we shall better illuminate certain reactions to these ancient practices. Likewise, perhaps Boswell would have been better served by recalling a certain tendency in himself, such as his own

---

p. 499. Hazlitt, William. "Pope, Lord Byron, and Mr. Bowles." In *The Collected Works of William Hazlitt: Fugitive Writings*, 11:486–507. London: J.M. Dent & Co., 1904.

20. See Walter Jackson Bate, *John Keats,* Belknap Press, 1979, p. 379.

21. Samuel Johnson, *The Rambler,* No. 2, Saturday, 24 March 1750. Reprinted in *Samuel Johnson: Selected Essays,* Penguin, 2003, p. 11.

22. "Remarks on Frazer's *Golden Bough,*" p. 127.

23. "Remarks on Frazer's *Golden Bough,*" p. 127.

propensity to doubt and to become "very uneasy from speculations in the abstruse and sceptical kind."[24]

And of course, Wittgenstein's own method for dealing with the painful muddles of philosophy was precisely *not* to seek more information of an empirical or theoretical nature. Rather, his approach was to offer a perspicuous representation of our linguistic practice that would enable us to "see the connections" between our uses of language clearly, thereby permitting confusions previously felt as problems to dissipate. As Wittgenstein puts it in a famous passage:

> [The problems of philosophy] are, of course, not empirical problems; they are solved, rather, by looking into the workings of our language, and that in such a way as to make us recognize those workings: *in despite of* an urge to misunderstand them. The problems are solved, not by giving new information, but by arranging what we have always known.[25]

"The work of the philosopher," Wittgenstein says, "consists in assembling reminders for a particular purpose."[26]

6.4.   Before returning to Hume's discussion of miracles with some of these ideas in mind, I would like first to explore Hume's perhaps least-read work on religion, *The Natural History of Religion*. Here, Hume seeks to locate the genesis of religious belief in the history of man and to discover "those principles," he writes, that "give rise to the original belief."[27]

For him, this is not the same as inquiring into "the principles of reason" that might best justify theistic beliefs. Hume writes as if the very best argument here is one from design—he calls this "the strongest proof"[28]—but he also believes that this argument is beyond the minds of "the vulgar."[29] He offers two reasons. First, those who advance an argument from design must appreciate "the glorious appearances of nature,

24. *Boswell in Search of a Wife, 1766–1769*, McGraw-Hill, 1956, p. 312.
25. *Philosophical Investigations*, §109.
26. *Philosophical Investigations*, §127.
27. David Hume, *Dialogues and Natural History of Religion*, J. C. A. Gaskin (editor), Oxford, 2009, p. 134.
28. *The Natural History of Religion*, p. 154.
29. *The Natural History of Religion*, p. 154.

the heavens, the air, the earth, his own organs and members; and would be led to ask, whence this wonderful scene arose."[30] But man, Hume says, was originally a "barbarous, necessitous animal"[31] and consequently not able to "observe the beauty of the work."[32] Second, the design hypothesis—namely, that of a supreme creator—is simply beyond the cognitive capabilities of the vulgar: "Such a magnificent idea," Hume writes, "is too big for their narrow conceptions."[33]

Instead of being able to appreciate "the beauty of the work," the glorious organization and regularity in the observed world, primitive man, driven by ignorance and fear, fixated instead on "disorders . . . prodigies . . . miracles."[34] The attentions of the vulgar were directed to singular disastrous events, and their energies were consumed by attempts to avert them. As Hume says in an arresting passage:

> Agitated by hopes and fears of this nature, men scrutinize, with a trembling curiosity, the course of future causes, and examine the various and contrary events of human life. And in this disordered scene, with eyes still more disordered and astonished, they see the first obscure traces of divinity.[35]

The way this comes about, Hume suggests, is that humans are naturally drawn to think that observable events are the work of hidden and intelligent forces. Humans, he writes, exhibit "[t]he universal propensity to believe in invisible, intelligent power, [which is,] if not an original instinct, [then] at least a general attendant of human nature."[36] And so he suggests that our ancestors naturally concluded that all the disorders of the world that plagued them were the products of hidden intelligent forces very much "like themselves."[37] And they further speculated, Hume says, that these "disorders" of nature, large and small, might be averted if only they could sufficiently placate the beings responsible for them. "The mind," Hume writes, "sunk into diffidence, terror, and

---

30. *The Natural History of Religion,* p. 136.
31. *The Natural History of Religion,* p. 136.
32. *The Natural History of Religion,* p. 142.
33. *The Natural History of Religion,* p. 142.
34. *The Natural History of Religion,* p. 154.
35. *The Natural History of Religion,* p. 140.
36. *The Natural History of Religion,* p. 184; see also p. 141.
37. *The Natural History of Religion,* p. 141.

melancholy, has recourse to every method of appeasing those secret intelligent powers, on whom our fortune is supposed entirely to depend."[38] This appeasement of "intelligent voluntary agents, like ourselves,"[39] naturally involved gifts and flattery, which the supplicants eventually came to believe were very well deserved. As the gifts mounted, so too did our ancestors' estimation of their recipients, until they judged them divine: "Men's exaggerated praises and compliments still swell their idea upon them; and elevating their deities to the utmost bounds of perfection, at last beget the attributes of unity and infinity, simplicity and spirituality."[40] So was born ritual and the belief in hidden agents of great power; that is, so was born religious practice and thought.

This is the gist of Hume's genetic explanation—his "natural history"— of religion, which he offers as an empirical hypothesis about the origins of religious belief and practice. Some will demur, however, for reasons that echo Wittgenstein's critical remarks about Frazer. Although Hume initially presents primitive man—this "barbarous, necessitous animal"— as a creature quite incapable of following fine philosophical reasoning, such as the argument from design, primitive man nevertheless is clearly imagined to be rational—indeed, to be endowed with a modicum of what philosophers call *practical rationality*, the ability to reflect on how one ought to behave if one is to promote one's own interests. Primitive man may be deluded in thinking that intelligent agents, rather like him, were acting behind the scenes, but given this belief and the desire for favorable natural events, the decision to propitiate these beings with praise and gifts is quite a reasonable one—anyone with a boss will understand it. The problem, however, is that this rationality is hard to keep in focus once we remember that primitive man regularly encountered circumstances in which things went well without any offerings having been made, and in which things did not despite offerings of gifts and songs of praise. It strains not so much credulity as intelligibility to imagine rational agents continuing over generations to engage in what they take to be beneficial practices in circumstances that give those agents plenty of reason to believe those costly practices to be ineffective.

---

38. *The Natural History of Religion*, p. 143.
39. *The Natural History of Religion*, p. 152.
40. *The Natural History of Religion*, p. 159.

Hume, like Frazer, was fascinated by religious belief. If Hume were not famous for his equanimous nature, one might even speculate that he was truly perturbed by the phenomenon of religious belief, for it was one to which he returned again and again in his writings. And like Frazer, his response was to tame it by offering an empirical hypothesis for its genesis in terms that were familiar to him—in this case, by showing how religious practice evolved from an exercise of our faculty of reason. This is obscured initially by the fact that Hume clearly means us to think the vulgar unreasonable in reaching their religious views. But they are unreasonable only insofar as their reasoning is premised on the false view that "invisible, intelligent powers" susceptible to blandishments are capable of actions that can ruin their lives. Given this view however, their propitiatory actions are eminently reasonable. At least, that is what Hume would like us to believe. For were he to have succeeded in showing this, he would have succeeded in offering an explanation for these practices and beliefs, one that makes them less alien by showing how they adhere to a familiar pattern of rational action.

In a sense, Hume would like to have it both ways. He would like to explain the genesis of religious beliefs in terms of a "train of thinking"[41] on the part of primitive peoples—that is, in terms of a process of practical reasoning that makes sense to us. But at the same time, he wants to be able to criticize their conclusions—in this case, presumably by criticizing alleged background assumptions about the existence of hidden intelligent agents that respond to flattery. There is nothing wrong with wanting to be able to do both. I worry that he has failed to do the first, however, for no beings we would happily deem rational would continue to engage in costly placatory activity in the face of random results. That simply is not what placatory activity looks like.

6.5.   Let us conclude by returning to our starting point, Hume's "Of Miracles." Here again, the focus is on the phenomenon of religious belief, in particular the fact that many people, including intelligent and educated people, believe in the occurrence of miracles deemed to be of religious significance. Hume's approach to such belief is to view it as often based on a valuable and ubiquitous method for arriving at

---

41. *The Natural History of Religion,* p. 154.

justified belief—namely, reliance on testimony. In general, this is as rational a method for forming justified beliefs about the world as any we possess. When Hume assimilates belief in miracles to testimony-derived beliefs about "ordinary historic facts,"[42] such as who was King of Scotland in 1500, he makes the acquisition of such beliefs explicable as an exercise of reason—explicable, but still subject to criticism. For the upshot of his argument in "Of Miracles" is that, in arriving at such beliefs by these means, errors of weighing are typically made.

In the current vein, perhaps we ought to be concerned about this assimilation. One might locate the concern by comparing it to Samuel Johnson's dismissal of Hume. Recall that Johnson thought Hume's discussion of little interest because the latter insisted on "taking the proposition simply." That is, Hume construed the believer in miracles to be justifying his belief through an inference from testimony that is comparable to our reasoning about "ordinary historic facts." Johnson did not challenge the intelligibility of this construal but instead claimed that it is of no interest, for most believers, he said, consider the relevant testimony in conjunction "with the doctrines in confirmation of which the miracles were wrought." Christians, Johnson may have thought, do not reason from testimony against the religion-free background that Hume imagined. Johnson does not question that it makes sense to imagine someone engaged in such reasoning; he just thinks that that is not what Christians in fact do.

By contrast, our concern here is with the very intelligibility of "taking the proposition simply." The inference to religiously significant miracles on the basis of testimony is, as Wittgenstein put it, so "exceedingly flimsy" that we ought to pause before we attribute it to anyone: nobody, one wants to say, could be that foolish.[43] To my ear, there is

---

42. Ludwig Wittgenstein, *Lectures and Conversations on Aesthetics, Psychology and Religious Belief,* Cyril Barrett (editor), California, 1972, p. 57.

43. Of course, Wittgenstein appreciates that people have wanted to claim just that—namely, that religious doctrines can be justified in the same way as "ordinary historic facts." He says that such a person is "a man who is cheating himself" (*Lectures and Conversations on Aesthetics, Psychology and Religious Belief,* p. 59). Presumably, Wittgenstein means that such a man, because he is gripped by a need to assimilate some of his convictions to others, presses into service a picture of justification that will not happily fit. In trying to satisfy his need for assimilation, he obscures from himself large differences and thereby cheats himself of this understanding. If the self-cheating is sufficiently successful, one might indeed lose a grip on the correct content to attribute to his words.

indeed something odd in concluding, as Hume does, that someone who infers thus is unjustified—not because there is an obvious error in Hume's analysis but rather because the patent flimsiness of the inference is too great to make sense of someone's taking it seriously.

Hume ends his essay with the cheeky remark that, in light of his discussion, it would take a miracle for "any reasonable person"[44] to believe that testimony on behalf of a miracle rendered acceptance of the miracle rational. But insofar as it would, then by Hume's own lights we have enormous reason not to attribute such a belief. Better to conclude that the individual who points to the testimony for miracles operates with a different conception of reasonableness or, less misleadingly, uses the term *reasonable* in a way that we do not quite understand. It is true that this person is not what we would call "reasonable" in drawing such an inference. But there is something peculiar in judging him or her, as Hume does, to be unreasonable.

Wittgenstein expresses a similar thought when he asks, speaking of those with religious beliefs:

> Am I to say they are unreasonable? I wouldn't call them unreasonable. "Unreasonable" implies, with everyone, rebuke.
> I would say, they are certainly not *reasonable,* that's obvious.
> Not only is it not reasonable, but it doesn't pretend to be.[45]

I draw from Wittgenstein the suggestion that there is no better proof that no one seriously makes the evidential judgments Hume challenges (whatever might be said)[46] than the fact that such judgments would be "more than ridiculous," nothing "that anyone could soberly argue"—in short (to appropriate Hume's words from another context), "so stupid."[47] Where Johnson expresses a lack of interest in Hume's conclusion because it concerns the rationality of believing the proposition when taken "simply," Wittgenstein deploys an insight, perhaps original to Hume himself, to question whether we could ever have grounds for attributing such a belief to anyone. From this perspective, Johnson is indeed as

---

44. "Of Miracles," in *An Enquiry Concerning Human Understanding* (critical edition), Tom L. Beauchamp (editor), Oxford, 2006, pp. 83–99; paragraph 41.
45. *Lectures and Conversations on Aesthetics, Psychology and Religious Belief,* p. 58; I have taken the liberty of eliding paragraph breaks, rearranging some remarks, and omitting others.
46. See footnote 43 above.
47. *Lectures and Conversations on Aesthetics, Psychology and Religious Belief,* p. 61; "Of the Dignity and Meanness of Human Nature," p. 84.

confused as Hume in thinking that it is an option to attribute to someone a belief in the proposition when taken simply, even if an option not well advised in the case of a believer like Johnson.

I have interpreted Hume as charging that a belief in miracles on the basis of testimony pulls the rug out from under itself. Here, we have another kind of self-undermining. The present objection to Hume is that his attribution to others of a belief in the proposition when taken simply is an attribution that undercuts itself. For to attribute such a conviction to someone is, Hume himself grants, to attribute a belief that "subverts all the principles of [the believer's] understanding."[48] And when confronted by such radical subversion, we lose all basis for attribution of belief in the first place.

But as mentioned before, it is not just that, in taking claims about evidence as Hume does, we court attributing an intolerable level of irrationality. It is also the case that so many trappings of, as we say, "believing on the basis of the evidence" are often not present in the context of religious beliefs. For instance, I believe on the basis of extensive evidence that someone will walk into Central Park in the next hour. This is a hypothesis that all my experience supports resoundingly—that my experience "proves," to use Hume's term. And yet, would I bet my life that it is a correct prediction? Would I even bet half of my assets? Now, compare this to someone who, as a result of reading the Gospel of Matthew, believes in the Last Judgment, in the sense that it regulates her entire life, that she sacrifices great pleasures on account of it, that she is prepared even to give up her life for it. Is this what forming a belief about the future on the basis of the evidence looks like? Imagine that you were informed that a blue ribbon panel of scientists had finally concluded its decade-long inquiry into the matter and announced that, in the distant future, everyone who ever lived will be dealt with "according to their works." Would you now radically change the course of your life, make all your decisions with this conclusion before your mind? Would you now be prepared to give up your life to be able to act from that prediction? We court mystification if we do not remain alive to the enormous differences between these cases.

But then what are we to say of someone who seems to express such a belief? When, for instance, Johnson suggests that testimonial evidence makes it reasonable to reaffirm the Christian doctrine, how are

---

48. "Of Miracles," paragraph 41.

we to take this suggestion? When he uses the words *proved* and *confirmation*, how are these to be understood? If not as Hume normally uses these words, for that would be to have Johnson take the proposition simply, then how?

The situation is a vexing one. If Johnson were to deploy these words very differently from the way we do in a wide range of cases, then we would have little hesitation in declaring that he was not speaking of proof or confirmation. Or, if he were to use the words very nearly as we do, only occasionally falling into something that we could happily judge to be an error or a confusion, then we might have no compunction in identifying what he calls "confirmation" with our own so-called notion. But we enter unsettling territory when we find both that there is a wide and significant overlap in our uses of this family of terms and yet also that Johnson employs them in different ways that cannot comfortably be chalked up to error, of which we want to say with Wittgenstein, "For a blunder, that's too big."[49] Here, we feel we can hold neither that Johnson employs our notion of evidence nor that he makes use of some wholly other notion. In such a circumstance, as Wittgenstein puts it, "My normal technique of language leaves me."[50]

The abnormality of the situation will be hidden from view so long as one thinks that it is acceptable to judge that Johnson's conception of confirmation is really just ours *except that . . .* and here we fill in the details of Johnson's views on the confirmation certain testimonies provide for the Christian revelation. There is really no more substance to this than there is to the claim that chess is really just checkers *except that . . .* or that an apple is really just an orange *except that. . . .* We might recall Wittgenstein's imagined patient who tells a doctor: "This thing that looks like a hand isn't just a superb imitation—it really is a hand." Is one tempted to think that this is just a piece of information *except that* it is spectacularly superfluous? Or rather, as Wittgenstein suggests, "Shouldn't I be more likely to consider it nonsense, which admittedly did have the form of a piece of information? . . . The background is lacking for it to be information."[51] So while there could of course be

49. *Lectures and Conversations on Aesthetics, Psychology and Religious Belief,* p. 62.
50. *Lectures and Conversations on Aesthetics, Psychology and Religious Belief,* p. 55.
51. *On Certainty,* G. E. M. Anscombe and G. H. von Wright (editors), Harper Torchbooks, 1972; §461.

circumstances in which we might say that someone's conception of confirmation is much like ours *except that* . . . , one might easily feel well beyond them when dealing with Johnson's judgments about the "proof" conferred by testimony on the Christian revelation and its attendant miracles.

Insofar as this is the case, Johnson's claim defeats our language (or the language of those who speak from outside the Christian doctrine). The situation can seem both to call for a particular description and to debar it. Our words fail us.

These kinds of failures are quite common, and they are often a source of philosophical perplexity. Responses to them vary enormously with individual sensibilities. One reaction is to ignore the warning bells, perhaps not to hear them at all, and to force our language onto the situation. Whether such a response garners philosophical attention and comes to seem attractive or interesting, as opposed to blindly or even willfully perverse, will depend in part on what work it generates. Philosophers, like most everyone, want to keep busy. An approach that provides tools that allow the formulation of seemingly tractable questions, interesting answers, and assessable arguments will often feel satisfying. And the bustle of activity can distract one's attention from any nagging discomfort induced by our unhappy uses of language.

Hume's reaction to claims by religious believers about the evidential significance of testimony is of this kind. He took their propositions simply, treating their claims about confirmation as completely on a par with those made by the scientist or the historian. Once this step was taken, his philosophical genius was unleashed to yield analyses and arguments that have absorbed readers for centuries. But in this last chapter, we have focused on his first, almost invisible step. And we have considered whether, in taking it, Hume set off on a brilliant walk down a dark path.

ACKNOWLEDGMENTS

Amherst College generously supported this work in many different ways. Portions of this book were originally presented as the 2011–12 Romanell–Phi Beta Kappa Lectures, an opportunity for which I remain thankful. I am also grateful to the Amherst College Library, the National Library of Scotland, the Library of the University of Edinburgh, and the British Library. And I am indebted to friends and family, ever-loving checks all.

INDEX